Thank you so much
for your support, Anne.

Hope you enjoy

'Survival Without Roots'- Book One.

Anna Anderson

Survival Without Roots

Memoir of an Adopted Englishwoman

Anna Anderson

First published in Great Britain in 2022 by Anna Anderson.

Copyright © Anna Anderson, 2022

First edition

A CIP catalogue record for this book is available from The British Library.

ISBN 978-1-7398883-0-5

Cover design: Nick Ball – www.nickballdesign.co.uk

Printed and bound in Great Britain by Imprint Services

For further information please contact the author:

Email: anna@annaandersonbooks.com

Website: www.annaandersonbooks.com

For Derek, my partner in crime.

Your support, encouragement and belief in my dream of becoming a published author means that my book is now a real book out there in the big, wide world.

Throughout each moment of self-doubt, you have offered me love and talked me into believing in myself again.

I could never have achieved this without you.

For Gwyneth, my lifelong friend.

You are not mentioned in this book as describing our adventures together since those days in the 'Brownies' would have become a book in itself.

Now, there's a thought ...

Thank you for always being there.

'Give me a child until he is seven,

and I will show you the man.'

Aristotle

'Music acts like a magic key, to which the most

tightly closed heart opens.'

Maria von Trapp

'Children should be seen and not heard.'

Margaret Mary Burton – my 'Mum'

Acknowledgements

My thanks go to ...

Kath Shadnia, for your unending support, advice and a constructively critical eye of my content when needed. You have been with me every step of the way and I will always remember that.

Jenny Williams, for proofreading with great skill, warmth and precision. You went 'above the call of duty' offering suggestions around my layout and storyline.

Nick Ball, for your beautiful cover designs and your patience with my numerous requests for alterations and tweaking.

'Local lads', Dave Dowson, Simon McCabe and Steve Hornsey, for kindly allowing me to use your magnificent photographs of Yarm-on-Tees and Staithes.

Christine Vickers, for your permission to include a photo of us in our younger days.

Alabama Rose Watson for your amazing pencil drawing of 'The Face'.

The 'guru' himself, Michael Heppell and your 'Write That Book' programme, without which my unfinished manuscript would still be gathering dust somewhere.

The members of the 'Write That Book' Masterclass '21/22, for your continuous stream of advice, support and encouragement covering all aspects of the never-ending process of getting my book 'out there'.

To you, the reader for buying my book. I hope you enjoy it and come back for more.

Finally, to my partner in crime, Derek. From a standing start, you have developed a wonderful website for me. Each day you have 'battered your head' to learn about the technicalities we had no idea even existed six months ago.

Mum's 'Mini'

In 1970, when I was sixteen, Mum acquired her first ever brand-new car.

Including a photo here will hopefully explain to my younger readers, the difference in size between the Austin 'Mini' of yesteryear and the BMW 'Mini' of today. It was positioned so low to the ground, it felt like you were almost scraping your bottom off the tarmac during each journey. The car's heater was either 'on' or 'off' with no 'in between' setting and the direction of the airflow could not be changed. The ash tray was simply a tiny, sunken metal box on top of the dashboard with a hinged grille. With the way my Auntie Freda chain-smoked, it was overflowing with ash in no time at all.

Bought for the princely sum of £587.00, it was a huge part of my life and is therefore mentioned many times in my story. Mum and her trusty orange 'Mini' took me on some of the worst journeys of my younger life.

This photograph reminds me that Mum could smile although it was only on rare occasions that she gave me the benefit of seeing her with a happy face.

Introduction to Me

There isn't any wonder

It's not a surprise

That I'm still learning

Who I am

I am of the two-headed variety. The first head is the *Me* that Mum tried to mould and manipulate as I grew up. The second head is the *Me* that rebelled after fourteen years of her control and undertook a never-ending search for my identity.

My upbringing, my moulded personality and the emotional wounds gathered along the way have influenced how I show myself and my emotions to the world.

I am adopted. I also have two adopted children, now in their thirties, and somewhere out there in the world we all share, there is a daughter who is mine. My own flesh and blood. A daughter that truly belongs to me.

I have a story that must be told, to help others unearth their resilience and to suggest to you that, no matter what life throws your way, you must become stronger after each throw hits its target because there is no alternative. If all becomes too much to endure, I say to you … write a book.

Writing my story was a long-standing itch I needed to scratch. It had to be done to pour out the pain of my life so far.

The therapy of pouring mountains of negative memories and emotions onto a page dulls the pain, stops it from consuming you and allows you to carry on with another day, with hope in your heart.

Little did I know, as I drowned in the sea of adopted emotions, that at seventeen I would give birth to a special little person of my own and would immediately be forced to give her up for adoption, for ever. Who would have thought that, later in life, adoption would come round to call again, and I would have the chance to bring up two precious little people: my two adopted children. Adoption has affected us all.

My book is written from an adopted person's point of view, as that is all I have ever known. Adopted and without identity, I have spent my life hovering on the edge of belonging, to anything or anyone. I see the world through the adoption cloud that's always there hanging above me, waiting to shroud me in insecurity and questioning. The cloud that reminds me I have never known the joy of belonging to someone through flesh and blood. I have no one that looks like me, talks like me, or thinks like me. I only have me. I am alone but I am strong.

Do not misunderstand me. In every country, there will be adoptions that have succeeded, and the adopted ones will have blossomed into belonging. My book is a personal story written from my perspective and nothing more.

Throughout my book, I refer to songs associated with various memories and powerful emotions in my life. Music has pulled me through; of that I am sure. Music has made me happy, made my heart skip a beat, made me sob and even transported me away from this world when it has been far too painful to bear.

If you have the time and the inclination, please listen to *my music* and you'll get to know me as I let you into my world. You'll be able to picture me singing as a young girl at the top of my voice with a sparkle in my eyes. The sparkle of happiness. Then as I grow older and the happiness fades, you'll be able to picture me struggling to join in with all sorts of lyrics and tunes without the tears spilling over and rolling down my face, as I sit quietly wondering who I am. The 'soundtracks of my life' are listed at the end of each chapter, and hopefully, they may reawaken memories for you, too.

One thing is certain. I am a complicated machine that frequently needs reassurance that all my moving parts are worthy of oiling and fixing and that I am also worthy of someone else's love and affection. This machine has had some hard hills to climb, some gaping chasms to fly over and some rough seas to endure. Yet up to this point in time, it has never broken down completely, merely gone off the proverbial rails on many occasions, in a detour away from reality, before getting back on track.

I wrote this book for myself. It had to be done to offload the pain and suffering and finally begin my healing process. I needed to explore my inner battles by telling the story of my journey through the first eighteen years of my life. I stand proud that I am here with my story started and I am determined I shall be here until its conclusion in my third book of the *Survival Without Roots* series.

I wrote this book for you, too. As you read my book, I hope it provides you with an understanding of the challenges myself and some other adoptees face in being brought up and feeling like an imperfect fit without identity. You may also find yourself saying, 'Oh, me too' – as you reflect on traumatic times in your own life. Sometimes it can help, knowing you are not alone in experiencing these confusing emotions and feelings. If I have survived, then so can you. Dig deep, grab hold of your determination, and you will find the strength to allow yourself to bounce back, begin to heal and quietly shine again. If you have always shone, be thankful that you have bypassed the sad times, the dark times and the wondering that some of us adoptees must endure.

Now it's your turn to engage. You'll provide the communication between us when you take time out to sit back, relax and turn the pages one by one, entering my world as it plods, careers and swerves through life. Thank you for being here.

('Music' – John Miles – 1976)

Introduction to Mum

This is the Mum who raised me and the lady I grew to despise. As she got older, she mellowed, and my love for her developed … or was it pity? Whatever it was, I knew I needed to care. She needed me, and I was there for her.

'She's not so good today. She didn't want her cornflakes and refused to get up,' Barbara said, as I walked towards the hall stairs in Park House, the care home where Mum had lived for the previous two weeks.

'Thank you, Barbara. I'll go and see if I can cheer her up. I thought I'd take her to the park if there's a wheelchair free this morning?'

'Yes, of course. Just bring her down when you're ready and buzz me. I'll come and help you get her in … and tell her it's fish and chips for lunch today. That'll please her.'

At Highfield, the care home Mum lived in before Park House, I arrived each day to see tears and frustration.

'I *hate* it here, Anne. I can't put up with it any longer,' and the tears escalated into sobbing as her frail body slumped further down in the chair by her bed, and she covered her face with her bony hands.

Kneeling in front of her and taking her hands in mine, I said, 'Mum, come and live with us and let us look after you.'

As happened every time I had mentioned her moving in with us, she raised her eyebrows and the stare said it all. She went back in time in her head.

'It wouldn't work. You know we can't live together. We'd be at each other's throats again.'

'That was a long time ago, Mum,' I said, knowing that arguing was pointless as it always had been. She had to win. She had to have control, even at ninety-one years old.

The staff at Park House were kind-hearted and dedicated. Within days of moving in, Mum's mood lifted dramatically. During her lucid moments, which were becoming less frequent, she was full of praise for her new companions, her carers – even the food was to her liking. Poor Mum. For years I despised her for all she had done and never imagined a day when I would feel sorry for her, but as she grew older and mellowed somewhat, we finally managed to get along. For the last twenty years, her sight had been failing to the point where all was a blur, and now dementia was invading her mind too, quietly taking it over.

I wonder if she'll know me today? I thought, as I climbed the stairs to her room. Opening the door, I was welcomed by the familiar rhythmic snoring that filled our house each night when I lived at home.

'Wake up Mum,' I whispered, as I knelt by her bed and cradled her hand in mine. Her eyes focused on me with full recognition and a weak smile crossed her face.

'I'm not well, Anne. I don't know what's wrong, but *I'm ready to go.* I've had enough of this life,' she said, her eyes pleading with me for release.

We'd had more cuddles in those last few weeks than in our entire life together and hearing those words made me pull her close and reassure her that all would be well. I didn't know what else to say, but I understood what she was trying to tell me.

Isn't life strange? The roles were reversing. On that fateful day at Park House, she was the child, and I was the parent offering her comfort.

Playing the role of the mum of old, I stood up and took control.

'What you need is some fresh air. I'll wrap you up well and we'll go to the park. It's a beautiful snowy morning out there and the sun's shining. Come on now. It'll do you good.'

She slipped into the abyss of dementia once more and glared at me, wondering who this person could be, bossing her about. Her head shook slowly from side to side like a rotating fan set on low speed.

'I don't want to go out today,' she said in a babyish voice as she pulled the paisley quilt cover up around her chin, pursing her lips and frowning at me. I took no notice. I was determined to get her out of that room and into the fresh air for a while. I was wrong to do so. I know that now.

Swaddled in a stripey blanket of red and green, I wheeled her towards the park. With her eyes shielded from the winter sun by her dark prescription glasses, she kept pulling her hat further down over her ears and complaining, 'It's cold … it's so cold, Anne.'

'Just ten minutes, then I'll take you back,' I said. 'I want you to hear the birds singing first, and you can guess which ones they are. We'll play for points. That'll be fun, won't it?'

Mum frowned again and fell silent. The frozen snow crunched against the wheels of her chair as we made our way towards the park, minutes along the street from the care home. Going through the iron gates we started our guessing game, and I knew she would win. In her garden, in years gone by, she adored enticing and feeding the blackbirds, the robins and any other breed that cared to visit her wooden bird table, anchored high on the garden wall to keep the rats at bay.

She often reminded me of the *rat factor* in life, saying, 'You're never more than three feet away from a rat. Remember that. It'll come in handy one day.' Up to now it never had.

The trees in the park glistened, with droplets of melting snow dripping from their branches, and Mum started to take an interest.

'Magpie,' she shouted, determined to outdo me.

'One-nil,' I answered, laughing.

Pushing her towards the 'Café in the Park', she chuckled at the excited voices of the toddlers as they ran to climb the steps of the small slide in the playground, in front of the cafe.

How things have changed, I thought. *Excitement was never allowed in our house.*

Lifting her head and twitching her nose she said, 'I can smell coffee.'

'Do you want one, Mum?' I asked.

'No! It's far too cold to be sitting outside drinking coffee, you silly girl.'

Don't let that get your back up, I told myself, slowly turning her chair around to head for the exit.

'Blackbird,' she said, pointing to a leafless old oak tree as we made our way back to the gates.

'Two-nil. Well done, Mum.'

The look that followed told me she was still lucid, and she was not enjoying being treated like a child.

A council worker with a leaf-blowing machine sporting an orange hi-vis jacket ambled towards us, propelling piles of multicoloured autumn leaves from the path onto the snow-covered grass.

'What's that noise?' Mum said, staring straight ahead.

When I explained, she sat bolt upright in her chair and slowly swung her head round to face me. Using one of her all-time favourite words and almost shouting, she said,

'That's *ridiculous*! What a waste of money. They'll only blow back onto the path again. Who on earth thought of that idea? Oh, it'll be the council. They've always been useless.'

Mum chuntered incessantly about the whole concept of leaf blowing all the way back to the care home. As I helped her into the lounge, some of the other residents cocked their ears as she told the tale of her *ridiculous* experience in the park. Those who were listening *and* lucid at that moment in time aired their views, agreeing with her. For the first time in my life, I was so proud that Mum was hanging on to the capability of persuading others to her point of view. She was well practised after all, and if persuasion failed then her next strategy would be to control. I knew that from experience.

Barbara stuck her head round the door of the lounge and announced,

'Fish and chips for lunch, ladies and gentlemen,' then paused before asking, 'and why's that?'

'Because it's Friday!' was the emphatic reply.

I bade my farewells to everyone and told Mum I'd see her the next morning.

'Enjoy your lunch, Mum,' I whispered in her ear, giving her a final cuddle, 'and don't work too hard in your exercise class this afternoon.'

With that parting sentence, I trudged through the snow back to my car with my throat aching.

No one needs to live to Mum's age, I thought. *Life can be cruel.*

'Hello, can I speak to Anne, please?' said the voice on the telephone. After confirming who I was, the news came flying down the line. Barbara's voice was barely audible as she told me Mum had suffered a massive stroke.

Trembling with emotion, her voice rattled on. 'Your mum thoroughly enjoyed her fish and chips, she really did. She kept on saying how *gorgeous* they were. "Better than any restaurant," she told everyone all the way through lunch. We'd just begun our exercise class when I spotted her sliding down in her chair and she couldn't talk or lift her arms. I'm so sorry, Anne,' she paused before adding, 'the ambulance has taken her to A & E at North Tees …'

Piecing the information together as quickly as I could, I headed, ridden with guilt, for our local hospital.

I shouldn't have taken her to the park ... it was too cold ... but at least she heard the birds. She'll have loved that.

('Blackbird' – The Beatles – 1968)

As I strode towards Ward 41, which I'd done each morning over the past week, the clearer the noise became. At first, it was like a distant burbling, winging its way along the corridor towards me. Getting closer, the volume increased. I felt sorry for whoever was in so much pain but relieved it didn't sound anything like Mum's voice.

Entering the ward, I smiled at the staff drinking their morning cuppas at the nurses' station and soon became aware that the noise was, indeed, coming from the direction of Mum's room. Fear grabbed me momentarily, and I froze. Then instinct took over. I rushed in to see her frail figure lying motionless in bed with a tube protruding from her nose, making its way up to a drip on a stand. It hadn't been there the day before.

Then the burbling began again.

'Jabber, jabber, yatter, yatter. Jibber, jabber, yitter, yatter.'

Walking towards her, I saw that her eyes were wide open, alert and drowning in a sea of fear. And she was alone. The machines were quietly beeping at the side of her bed, monitoring her blood pressure, oxygen levels and the like.

Sister Julie had told me during my visit the day before that she and another nurse were going to attempt to insert a nasogastric tube up Mum's nose and down her throat to feed her, as she had been unable to swallow since her massive stroke the previous weekend. They had tried twice before, but Mum, ever determined, somehow succeeded in pulling out the tube on both occasions before they could take an aspirate reading. A successful reading would confirm that the tube was correctly positioned in her stomach and not in her lungs. An X-ray would complete the safety check and feeding could begin.

'Jabber, jabber, yatter, yatter. Jibber, jabber, yitter, yatter.'

Complete nonsense was pouring from Mum's lips but the rise in intonation at the end of every sentence, accompanied by the silent screams, and the look of absolute panic in her eyes, alerted me to the fact that something had changed on this sunny Saturday morning of March 29th 2009.

Something was wrong.

Taking her cold, clammy hand in mine, I glanced at the gerbera pot plant on her bedside table, which I'd presented to this confused version of Mum on Mother's Day – the previous Sunday. Once again the flowers had wilted, soulfully hanging their scarlet heads as they'd done every morning since then, and every morning I'd watered them after saying my 'Good Morning's to Mum. Each time, and within an hour, the flowers slowly raised their heads as if to say they too were fighting back and defeating death. The gerbera's daily resurrection became a meaningful and much-needed signal that Mum would follow suit and survive, just as the gerbera was.

After watering it on this occasion, I sat beside Mum stroking her forehead and listening to her babbling while watching her frightened eyes locking onto mine. With each caress, I expected a nurse to walk in, to explain what had changed overnight. Their duty of care made me believe someone would come soon. It was not to be.

Leaving Mum's side with the words, 'I'll be right back,' I marched towards Sister Julie who was still finishing her morning cuppa. Not prepared to wait for her to look up, I said, 'Can you tell me what's wrong with Mum today?'

Sister Julie explained that at eleven o'clock the previous night, the process of feeding Mum through the tube had begun. After a successful aspirate reading, a junior doctor had double-checked the X-ray results to show the tube was correctly placed in her stomach.

Even though I believed Sister Julie to be a competent nurse, I questioned the fact that all was well, and the frantic babbling coming from Mum as we reached her bedside consolidated my fears.

Sister Julie assured me the babbling was a good sign and showed that Mum was more alert and interacting.

'You're alright, Margaret, aren't you?' she asked Mum, barely looking at her.

How on earth could Mum answer that one? I wasn't convinced. Glancing at the gerbera for reassurance, it showed no sign of recovery and, like its flowers, Mum's health was failing.

Why's this happening? I wondered, as Sister Julie left the room. *She's been doing really well.*

Taking Mum's hand, I homed in on the plant and silently confided in it.

It's the tube. I know it's the tube. There's something wrong.

The gerbera listened but did not answer.

After her admission to hospital the previous weekend, Mum had rallied, and two days later she had been moved to Ward 41, the general stroke unit. Her progress was remarkable, and the nurses were astounded as they carried out tests to assess her understanding. Mumbling her way through short sentences, she was able to make absolute sense to everyone who chose to listen carefully enough.

She progressed to sitting up and, with support from the nurses, was able to swing her legs unaided to the side of her bed, ready to be helped into a chair for the day. As time passed, she became increasingly mobile and also extremely verbal, reverting to her old ways of showing strength and determination by trying to control and shame everyone into action. This showed in the words she chose to use and the way she delivered them to the world. The words were not necessarily the kindest words and, in the following few days, I noticed many of the staff began to back off from communicating with her unless it was within their specific bounds of duty. They were avoiding her.

I received the brunt of her complaints about the staff, which she voiced at full volume, and was also told – in no uncertain terms – in front of everyone on Ward 41, that I'd always been the imperfect daughter and an utter disappointment to her.

I took it all on the chin, or pretended to, as I tried to forgive what she was saying. It was happening involuntarily, I told myself, as in her lucid moments she knew there was little time left for her to speak her mind. After all, it was nothing new. All my life, nothing I tried to do had been good enough for Mum.

'You never get it right.'

'You're such a disappointment, Anne.'

The year before her hospital admission, this 'disappointment of a daughter' noticed the warning signs as her mum's health started to fail. She sold her precious little semi-detached house in County Durham, moved back to where she had been raised and moved into rented accommodation. Dragging all her most treasured possessions with her, the 'disappointment of a daughter' chose to do this, to be close to her mum and take care of her. Geographically speaking, of course. Any other type of closeness was an impossibility and always had been.

Four days after Mum was moved to Ward 41, I arrived at around nine in the morning, acknowledged the multitude of staff at the nurses' station and walked into the ward to be with her for the day. She wasn't there. Her bed had been stripped and remade and was all ready for the next patient who had suffered the horrific and life-threatening condition known as a stroke. Time stood still as I stared at the empty bed.

A shiver ran through me as I processed split-second possibilities before I flew to find a member of staff. The first person I spotted was a tall, slovenly-looking healthcare assistant and her reaction to my worried enquiry made my blood boil.

'Where's my mum? Where's Mrs Burton?' I blurted out, pointing to the empty bed.

A drawling, monotone voice answered me.

'Mrs Burton … let me think … well, I'm not sure,' and looking into the distance, she came to a full stop. End of conversation. There was no offer to go and ask someone about Mum, nor a scrap of interest in finding out where she had gone.

I was fuming but remained calm as I knew I must. Looking straight at her, I said,

'Can we go and find someone who'll know where she is and can we do it right now, please?'

Sister Julie happened to be close by and, seeing me marching towards her in front of the healthcare assistant, she promptly took me to one side. With her voice almost a whisper, she said, 'We've tested Mum for C. difficile and it's come back positive, so we've had to move her to a room of her own, well away from the other patients. I'm sure you understand, it's the best for everybody.'

'What's C. difficile?' I asked, repeating the words and trying to take it all in.

'It's a highly contagious bacterium and moving her reduces the risk to everyone.'

Looking back at the empty bed I gathered my thoughts before asking, 'How did she get it?' but Sister Julie was already walking away.

Whether Mum ever had C. difficile, I cannot say, as it was not logged in the medical notes which I requested from the hospital in the following weeks.

Could it have been because she was too much trouble to have in the general ward and was causing a little too much fuss?

Whatever the reason for moving her to a room of her own, that sunny Saturday was a turning point in the long life of Mum. She continued to babble constantly and kept reaching for the tube as if she knew it was harming her, but her coordination had gone, and the tube stayed in place. I held her hand and stroked her head trying to give her some peace and reassurance.

Speaking softly, I said, 'It's okay, Mum, leave it alone,' using words anyone would have said when they don't know what to say or what to do.

I glanced at the gerbera plant, willing it to be showing some kind of revival, but the heads remained bowed. I knew it was a bad omen.

I tried to work out how to communicate with Mum as I couldn't bear to see the overwhelming terror in her eyes as she fixed her gaze on me once more. I knew that she was trying to tell me something and I felt utterly helpless.

Let's try this then, I thought, *after all, it can do no harm.*

'Mum, are you frightened?' I said, hoping a miracle would take place and she would sit bolt upright and answer me in her usual condescending manner, with the words, 'Of course I am, you silly girl. Wouldn't you be if you were me?'

Although I'd asked the question, I knew there was no chance of a reply. The only muscles functioning properly were her eye muscles. Then a light-bulb moment flickered in my head. Still holding her hand, I offered her a way of telling me what was wrong.

'Okay, Mum. Let's try this. If you're frightened … blink twice.'

Slowly and on cue, Mum blinked twice, and a tear slid down her left cheek. Fear enveloped us both and I held her as tightly as I dared. Gently releasing my hold on her and feigning calmness, I slid out of the room to find Sister Julie and tell her what had occurred. She listened to my tale without conviction, stepped back, offered a smile and said, 'It was probably a coincidence. Don't worry so much. At least she's interacting with you.'

Once again, I felt my blood starting to boil and my body tense up as no one was listening to me. If there was any possibility that those two blinks of Mum's meant she'd understood the question and had managed to answer in her own way, then surely that needed to be investigated by a doctor – and investigated quickly. I stood my ground and suggested this to Sister Julie, who replied, 'It'll be Monday before anything can be done. The only doctors on duty over the weekend are junior doctors, and they'll be busy looking after patients in two other wards as well as this one.'

Unbelievable! I thought.

All her working life, Mum had paid into the NHS system and because she was now an old lady of ninety-one, she was not a priority. I knew I was fighting a losing battle. However, in confronting Sister Julie and getting her back up, I wasn't helping Mum to get the best treatment she deserved. What a sad state of affairs.

As our conversation ended and Sister Julie went about her duties, I spotted Caroline, a retired nurse and the daughter of one of my Mum's lifelong friends. Walking back with her into Mum's room, she took one look at her and said, 'She's dehydrated. Her lips are severely cracked.' She went straight to the sink and filled a glass with water, which she dabbed on Mum's lips with a tissue, telling me I should repeat the procedure every half hour.

'What if the water goes down her throat?' I said, 'She can't swallow.'

'As long as none of it goes in her mouth, she'll be fine,' Caroline replied.

She then produced a tube of Burt's Bees lip balm from her handbag and suggested that, along with the dabbing, I should coat Mum's lips with it each hour.

'It's the best lip balm, Auntie Margaret,' she said, leaning over Mum, 'It will help your lips to feel much better.' Still babbling away, Mum slowly shifted her gaze to look at Caroline, without any recognition of who she was.

I felt ashamed. Why hadn't I thought of this, and more to the point, why were the nurses not doing it as a matter of course?

I asked Caroline her opinion on the incessant babbling and told her about the amazing 'two blinks' answer that happened shortly before she arrived. She tried to reassure me by saying, 'Even if she's frightened, and anyone would be in her situation, the babbling must be a good sign. It shows she's alert so try and stop worrying so much.'

As Caroline obviously knew her stuff, I held on to the hope that she was right. After sitting with Mum and chatting away, she stroked Mum's hand and said her goodbyes. I picked up the glass of water, staring at Mum's cracked lips. I couldn't do it. I was scared. *What if I make her choke?* I thought, *it could kill her.*

I opened the door to Mum's room and beckoned a nurse, explaining what Caroline had said, and asked her to sponge Mum's lips during her half-hourly checks.

'It's alright. You can do it, as long as you're careful,' was her abrupt reply.

'*So what are you here for?*' I wanted to shout, but somehow I bit my tongue. The look I gave the nurse, however, was brimming with disdain and she saw it, received it well and left the room, without sponging Mum's lips I have to add. Now it was most definitely up to me.

Each episode of the dabbing went well, and after coating Mum's lips for the final time, I left earlier than usual on that sunny Saturday, as I knew she must be exhausted. Hugging her ever so gently, I squeezed her hand twice hoping that two of anything had become an unwritten code between us and leant back over her, saying, 'See you tomorrow, Mum. I'll be here bright and early to spend the day with you. Sleep well.'

In amongst the babbling, a second miracle took place in that single room within Ward 41, as she squeezed my hand back … twice.

'Well done, Mum. Oh Mum, you clever thing! You squeezed my hand. You squeezed my hand … twice!'

Only Mum could give me the look that followed and without a doubt it said, 'Stupid girl … of course I did.'

On my way past the nurses' station, I repeated my request for Mum's mouth to be dabbed and coated and asked the nurse on duty to write it on Mum's treatment plan. It was clear to her that I was intent on making sure Mum had the best chance of recovery. Since she could see I was not about to move on until she agreed, she reluctantly wrote down my request, without any kind of smile or acknowledgment.

I walked back along the corridor towards the car park, blinking away the tears. Picturing the hand-squeezing miracle gave me comfort and hope, and I tried to put my doubts of the day to one side.

On reaching home, my partner suggested popping out for a quiet drink, if only for an hour. I jumped at the chance, as my neck was like a rod, still waiting for the welcome crack to release the tension and worry that had built up in me.

Ten minutes before we were due to leave, our plans changed dramatically when the house phone rang. Answering it, I heard Sister Julie's voice at the other end of the line simply stating that 'an incident' had occurred with Mum and they needed us to go back there immediately.

'Is she alright?' was my initial response.

I pressed for more information, but Sister Julie held firm, only saying that she had arranged an emergency meeting which would begin as soon as we arrived.

Incident … Emergency meeting … the words hit me in a blur and I did not understand. She would say no more but the calmness in the tone of her voice failed to cover up the fear she was desperately trying to hide, and I knew something horrific had happened, as I suspected throughout that sunny Saturday in 2009.

We raced back to the hospital, not knowing what to expect …

('Say Something' – James – 1993)

1

In the Beginning

I may grow up to be agoraphobic. I may need to become an alcoholic to cope with the agoraphobia and the suffering it causes me. The alcoholism will fuel my agoraphobia and I will spiral into depression because I am an agoraphobic and an alcoholic. The cycle will continue spinning and then I will die. I know not yet if this will come true.

('Que Sera, Sera, Whatever Will Be, Will Be',
Doris Day and Frank de Vol–1956)

On January 26th 1954, I came into this world in the most usual way: head first, from a mother's womb. From the beginning, I was rejected and cast aside with a label of 'unwanted'. That is a fact and has been for sixty-seven years now. I was born in Scarborough General Hospital in North Yorkshire, the best county in England. Memories are non-existent, but I am sure that not many rushed to say, 'Hello little one, welcome to the world.'

Three life-changing events took place in the sixth week of my life. Well, let me rephrase that. The same event took place, but I have been told on good authority that it happened in three spectacularly different ways. Confused? Wait a while and I will explain.

('Rat Trap'–The Boomtown Rats–1978)

Let's go back in time to the year of 1953: the year of our Queen's coronation, and the year before my birth.

Close your eyes and imagine an ancient market town in North Yorkshire surrounded on three sides by a horseshoe-shaped river, the River Tees. A town called Yarm, old enough to be mentioned in the Domesday Book of 1086. A pretty town with a wide, cobbled high street flanked by Georgian architecture, two hundred and forty miles north of London. Cross south over the old stone bridge spanning the river which marks the border between County Durham and North Yorkshire.

Take a walk round the corner into the High Street and observe how peaceful the town looks. Only a few treasured vehicles with chrome bumpers shining, parked randomly on the cobbles. Look along the left-hand side of the High Street and you will spot the Dutch-style town hall. Listen carefully as its clock strikes the hour, often drowned out by a steam train billowing thick black smoke as it thunders slowly across the viaduct which towers above the town. Head along the cobbles towards the Town Hall and, when you get there, you will be slap-bang in the middle of Yarm-on-Tees, the place destined to become my hometown and shape my future. A town with a population of two thousand and a feeling of protection within its community.

Come off the cobbles and visit the many individual shopkeepers who will be truly pleased to see you, as day after day they offer personal service with a smile.

Focus further now and join the daily life of one of those smiling shopkeepers. A shopkeeper, unaware of the words 'supermarket', 'self-service' and 'just-in-time accounting'. A greying, middle-aged and bespectacled grocer in a starched, white knee-length coat, trying to make ends meet in his high-class shop and smiling all the while, to hide his incessant worrying.

View of Yarm-on-Tees (Simon McCabe Photography)

Grocer Sandy is his name and his shop front at 16 High Street proudly bears the logo *W.S. Burton,* in blue and gold lettering. William Saunders Burton, or simply Sandy. Sandy the gentle grocer. A man with the most frightening of illnesses.

Go with him at the end of the day and, with his shop shut for the night, wearily climb the stairs that lead to the first floor of his home above the shop. Sit down with him for five minutes as he tries to unwind in the front lounge, gazing abstractedly at the images on the black-and-white television portraying the last five minutes of *Muffin the Mule.* Each evening he must justify his viewing choice to his hard-faced wife when she calls through from the kitchen. He sighs, but his reply and patient tone never falter.

'The *Six O'Clock News* is on soon,' he says.

Sit and watch *The News* with him, listening to the presenters with their middle-class voices pouring from the screen. Middle-class voices in an aspiring middle-class home. Watch Sandy silently worry that today was another day of little profit, while he waits for his dinner to be served by his good lady wife, Margaret. A strict and matter-of-fact lady with a good heart but unsure how to use it. A social climber of Yarm-on-Tees, who expects perfection from everyone, in every way, at all times.

'Dinner's ready. Come on now, Sandy, before it gets cold.'

Join Sandy and Margaret in the back kitchen as they eat their dinner, listening to the BBC World Service on the huge, mottled brown wireless, sitting on the sideboard next to them, with yet more middle-class voices pouring from its single speaker. Stay with them until after dinner and help them with the washing up, which must be done immediately after that last mouthful of dessert is swallowed. No time to savour the meal or relax and chat for a while.

'Otherwise, I couldn't settle, Sandy. What if we get visitors and we haven't tidied up?'

Agree wholeheartedly with Sandy, as he says to himself that they never get visitors apart from on a Monday, when Margaret's mother comes for dinner, before rushing off to the local whist drive in the Catholic church hall.

Follow them to the lounge and spend an evening with them, as their favourite programmes leap out from the screen of their new television set – a marvel of technology. Try to keep warm by the coal fire, doing its best to diminish the draught pouring through the two rotting, high, sash windows, and under the lounge door. Look at Sandy's furrowed brow as his mind drifts away from the programme he is sharing with his wife; flitting back and forth between ideas, wondering how to make a profit the next day so that he can order more stock for the shop.

Maybe I can start charging for deliveries? Maybe I can give customers special offers every week?

Watch Sandy straighten in his chair, as the all too familiar tightness in his chest kicks in, telling him an angina attack is on its way. The worry has taken control, and only the tiny white heart tablets can ease the pain and allow him to carry on to yet another day of smiling service for his valued customers. A man with the kindest of hearts whose only ambition in life is to protect his wife and give her the middle-class opportunities she so desires. A man who can't quite work out, yet, how to do that.

Daily life in their shop and the enormous home above it was an unending financial struggle. A huge three-storey Georgian property built in 1760, with dark, dank warehouses spanning the entire width at the rear and the building cried out for love and attention.

Dry rot ran amok throughout. Sandy's solution was to 'spot the rot', then hammer nails around the edge of old family-size biscuit tin lids, securing them to the offending areas, hoping for a day when he could afford to seek a proper solution. For now, he finished the job by throwing oddments of frayed carpet on top and praying that all would be well. Along with the dry rot, the house at 16 High Street was also filled with high emotion, soon to bubble over for the shopkeeper and his wife. For months now, they had been waiting for a telephone call that would change their lives for ever. A call that would stretch their finances even further for a good many years to come, yet a call that would fulfil their dreams.

2

The Telephone Call

One Thursday evening in late January 1954, Grocer Sandy locked and bolted the shop door at around half past five. Closing time was not set in stone. It was dependent upon last-minute customers turning up, knowing they would be given the same warm welcome as the first customer of the day, even though the fatigue was taking over. With the shop door secured, he heaved a sigh of relief and carried the till drawer through to the small back office where he sat down at his roll-top desk, deftly counted the takings of the day and tried to balance his books.

His assistant, Vic, a short ageing spiv with slicked-back, curly greying hair and a pockmarked nose, washed down the delicatessen counter, cleaned the bacon slicer until it gleamed and topped up the enormous, red, coffee-grinding machine with more fragrant coffee beans, making ready for the next day. Then he 'put up' the orders, ready for those far-flung farmers' wives, who preferred to receive their goods personally, courtesy of Sandy's free delivery service.

The evening before, Grocer Sandy had wondered about the possibility of charging them, but he knew in his heart he would never do it. He was too kind to take such drastic action, even though free deliveries were dreadful for profit.

His 'loyal' assistant diminished profits even further on delivery days. After adding the relevant perishable items to the cardboard boxes containing each order, he regularly sneaked in a few bits for himself and his close relatives. Best back bacon, home-cooked ham, eggs and the occasional succulent slice of fresh salmon found their way into another box which he promptly hid from view in the delivery vehicle, parked in the back yard behind the shop. Vic dropped off his pilfered provisions first, then carried on to deliver to the farmers' wives and partake in any refreshments offered. This perk of the job went on for years, undetected.

Grocer Sandy and his assistant went their separate ways that Thursday evening and once again, Sandy wearily climbed the stairs. After *The News*, he and Margaret ate their dinner in the back kitchen as usual, keeping warm from the heat of the coke-fired Aga.

Just the two of them were sitting there, along with Rex – their beautiful cocker spaniel puppy – who was a welcome addition to the family. Rex hovered at Sandy's feet, just in case he dropped a discreet morsel of food, accidentally on purpose, while Margaret was busy talking or immersed in listening to the wireless. Sooty, their skinny black cat and the world's best mouser, put in an appearance after scratching incessantly at the warehouse door behind the kitchen, demanding to be let in. She proceeded to ignore them all and contented herself with snuggling up on the old, worn 'clippy' mat in front of the Aga, knowing that the humans would feed her after their dinner.

The huge house above the shop took up the first and second floors. It had never known such luxury as central heating and there was the lack of enough love between them to keep Sandy and his wife warm. She was incapable of letting go, of having a right royal laugh about anything; incapable of putting her arms around her worn-out, worried husband to welcome him home at the end of yet another day of small profit at the shop. Instead, she delighted in taking control at the dinner table, launching into endless suggestions about how to make their shop viable, so she could climb another rung of the social ladder in Yarm-on-Tees. At the end of each day, Sandy's wish was to put the shop to the back of his mind and enjoy his wife's company, see her smile for once and, of course, enjoy his well-cooked dinner and dessert.

This was the normal routine in the life of the shopkeeper and his wife, followed by the tidying up, and then they could retire to the lounge overlooking the High Street, above their precious shop.

That evening, Margaret stoked up the coal fire and switched on the television. They settled themselves down, sitting separately. Sandy, head back and trying to relax in an armchair, and Margaret, bolt upright in one corner of the three-seater brocade sofa of which, lately, she had often remarked, 'It'll need to be changed before next Christmas when Doris comes.'

Another worry was thrown onto Sandy's ever-growing mountain of worries. He was sure that his sister would understand if it was the same sofa as last Christmas, but he said nothing, thinking, *What's the point?*

Talk of new sofas was soon forgotten, however, as their evening routine was about to be changed for ever.

Fast forward half an hour, and the old-fashioned black telephone started to tinkle in the background. Whenever this had happened over the previous few months, two hearts had begun to race and the adrenalin had flowed as they wondered if this could be the most important telephone call of their lives together. A call that would change everything. A call to the house in the High Street, waiting for a baby. A baby perfect in every way, who would grow up without the problems attributed to the never-ending debate of nature versus nurture. A baby waiting to be adopted, who would be so grateful for a new life and the opportunities that went with it and who would fit into the little family, without argument.

Sandy got out of his chair and, as fast as his heart would allow, rushed over to the other side of the lounge, took a deep breath and lifted the telephone receiver apprehensively to his ear.

'Hello, Eaglescliffe 3216. Sandy Burton speaking.'

His jaw dropped as he listened in amazement to the news that poured down the line, offered by the voice of a social worker from the Durham Diocesan Adoption Society, delegated to deal with their case. A case that had involved meeting after meeting, during which Sandy and Margaret had been thoroughly grilled in order to prove they were of impeccable character and would make ideal parents. The social worker explained that a baby girl had been born two days beforehand in Scarborough General Hospital. A healthy baby, with all her limbs intact. She would be ready to be transported to her new life at six weeks old, and Sandy and Margaret had been chosen to be her new parents.

The voice continued, 'The next step is for you to sign all the official paperwork and we can set a date after that for you to meet your new baby.'

Sandy listened carefully, staring at Margaret who was pacing backwards and forwards across the lounge, as he tried to take it all in. The voice signed off, and for a moment he stood frozen to the spot, receiver still in hand, with his heart pounding. Putting down the phone with a nervous clatter, he relayed the news to his waiting wife with tears of joy in his eyes, and Margaret, for once, let go. They held on to each other and sobbed, knowing that now they would be *normal* like everyone else. No more whispered murmurings from family and friends about their childless state, 'After all, they've been married for twelve years and there's no sign yet.'

No more wondering from them all if Rex the spaniel and Sooty the cat were substitutes for a child. What Sandy and Margaret didn't envisage on that special Thursday evening was that the whispered murmurings would not cease, but simply change direction and instead centre around the horrific dangers of adoption and *bad blood* entering the family.

'What's bred in the bone will come out in the flesh.'

For now though, the rest of the family received the news with polite and proper comments and even offered to help transform one of the bedrooms on the second floor overlooking the High Street.

In the following few weeks, excitement filled the huge house along with mild panic, anticipating the addition to Sandy and Margaret's 'one dog, one cat' family. Three of Sandy's sisters arrived complete with their pinnies and paint, and the transformation of the nursery began.

February arrived, and so did the gift of a cot and all the things that a six-week-old baby girl might need, and which most parents have nine months to ponder on and accumulate. The red-letter day was written in huge capitals on Sandy and Margaret's kitchen calendar; the day when they would meet their baby girl for the first time and bring her home for ever. The countdown had begun ...

In the second week of March, that day finally dawned, and the shopkeeper and his wife left 'Vic the Spiv' in charge of the shop and set off on a journey that seemed never-ending. A journey that would see them as a family without a child for the last time. All spruced up with the shopkeeper's shoes perfectly polished and hair Brylcreemed back, his wife wearing her brand-new tweed suit, matching hat and gloves, they began their journey towards a new life. Bound for Scarborough, the miles crawled by as they babbled nervously in the front of their old, green Morris Traveller. An empty, wicker Moses basket lay on the back seat, waiting to accommodate the special baby they were on their way to collect.

Thank goodness they were familiar with the town and knew the whereabouts of the hospital. Sandy's well-to-do sisters and their families often stayed in the magnificent Grand Hotel on the seafront and the couple from Yarm had visited them there for the day, on numerous occasions.

As they approached Scarborough, their excitement was replaced with trepidation: *What if it all goes wrong and there's no baby waiting for us? What if the real mother has changed her mind? Is she allowed to do that?*

So many questions filled their heads during those last few miles, but they didn't voice them, each trying to stay calm. Eventually, the hospital façade came into view and they gave each other one last look, took a deep breath, and Sandy parked the car. His heart was thudding, and he took the precaution of popping a tablet into his mouth, just to be on the safe side. On this occasion, Margaret didn't question his action, understanding the need.

In my story so far, we have a shopkeeper, a wife, a dog and a cat. Now we must change our perspective.

Let's carry on our reading with a new adoptive dad being introduced to us, instead of simply a shopkeeper and a new adoptive mum, instead of merely a wife. The dog and the cat shall remain, and of course a baby girl will join the story. A baby girl I've known for sixty-seven years and grown up with. I have questioned her actions on occasion, stared in disbelief at the choices she has made and been at the core of things she has had to go through. She is a girl I have never quite felt at home with or loved at all – until now, in my later years.

The profound impact that being *the chosen one, the adopted one, the 'should be perfect' one* has had, on my personality and life choices, is immeasurable. My decisions have affected my life without a doubt, but that is because of the way my personality has been moulded and so we come full circle.

('Walkin' Back to Happiness' – Helen Shapiro – 1961)

('Bad to the Bone' – George Thorogood and The Destroyers – 1982)

3

The Passing over of the Baby

On Good Authority (Version One - 1958)

When I was three years old, Mum and Dad told me I was adopted and, although I had no real understanding of what that meant, the word had been introduced into my life. And that's all it was, just a word. In a way, as time went by it explained why Mum was always cross with me and didn't seem to love me or enjoy having me around. Thankfully my dad was different.

He showed me love with his smiles and hugs and each day, in some little way, let me know he was over the moon that I was his little girl.

I asked him to tell me his romanticised 'Version One' time and time again, with increased understanding as the years passed. I loved scrambling up onto Dad's knee to snuggle into his shirted chest and see his brown eyes smiling at me, while his deep, pipe-smoking voice told me how that important day in Scarborough had unfolded. With his strong arms wrapped around me, I listened to him while tracing the furrows on his forehead and believed for a while that I was very, very special.

Suddenly I became more than one baby ready for adoption. I became many babies cooing and gurgling in the long hospital ward, hoping to be chosen.

'Your Mum and I were told by the nurse to have a walk down the ward and see which baby girl we would like to take home with us, to keep for ever. The ward was noisy, and we walked past all the cots with babies in them, until we saw you. You had such big, blue eyes, curly blonde hair and a huge smile and you shone like the sun [as if I had some kind of brilliant aura around me]. I started to cry because I was so happy; I looked at your Mum through my tears and said, "That's The One". I picked you up and cuddled you, and you felt like mine straight away. You were such a good girl, Tish, and you slept all the way home.'

So endeth my dad's version of events, which I still prefer to think of as the true version, although I never understood until later in life how anyone can cry and be happy at the same time.

'Tish' was his nickname for me from as early as I can remember and, as I got older, I christened him 'Tosh'. My Tosh. Tish and Tosh: two people who adored being together even though we were not bound by blood. Although it was never voiced aloud, we both knew that our happiest times were the times when we were together, without Mum.

On Good Authority (Version Two - 1958)

Mum, being much less of a romantic and not one for straying away from the facts, told me a different story. She offered it to me without a knee to climb on, without the hint of a cuddle and this version was offered only once in my life.

'When your dad and I got to Scarborough, we parked the car and straight away we saw a smartly dressed lady standing on the steps at the front of the hospital. She was holding on to a tiny baby. She was standing next to a tall lady. She passed the baby over to the tall lady and walked away. Your dad and I went over to the tall lady with the baby and she passed you over to us. You are so lucky that we chose you.'

After she told me her version, she often reminded me that the only people who knew I was adopted were the three of us, along with my relations.

'There's no need for anyone else to know,' she would say, lowering her voice, as if it was something I should be ashamed of from the start. In my head, secrecy and the word 'adoption' became intertwined, stirred around and mixed like a witch's brew, and I knew I must never tell *anyone*.

On Good Authority (Version Three - 2000)

'It was at a railway station. It was a dark, rainy night and it broke my heart.'

No matter how and where the passing over took place, my new life began at six weeks old. A name change occurred shortly after. *Pauline*'s identity ceased to exist and I morphed into *Margaret Anne*, named after two English princesses in the 1950s.

('Survival' – Yes – 1969)

4

A New Start

Yarm-on-Tees is the wonderful little market town where I grew up, and the place where so many years of reflective questioning took place. When I was three years old, a vast Georgian merchant's house, at 16 High Street, became my new home. In the photograph below, it is the closest house on the right-hand side with the shop awning lowered and two cars parked immediately outside.

A view of the High Street as it was in 1960

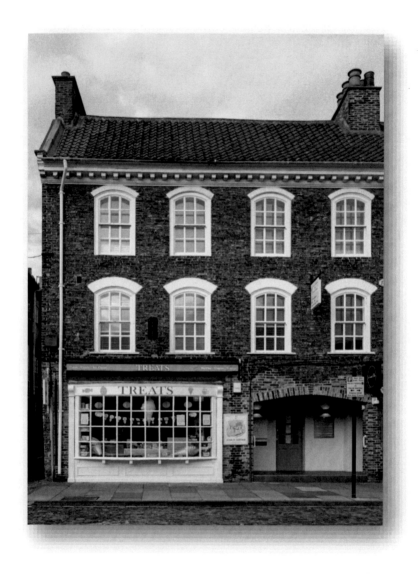

How 'our side' of my new home, with the shop underneath, looks in 2022 (Dave Dowson Photography).

The whole building was strange. It was divided into two separate residences with a partition wall running from the second-floor ceiling right down to the ground floor, and each side of the dividing wall had its own staircase creating 'our side' and 'the other side'. In the photo above, 'our side' is pictured.

On each of the first and second floor landings, an internal door allowed access from our side to the other side, although both were permanently locked. Dad rented out the other side to the Best family. On the ground floor, Mrs Best ran a café, simply called 'The Café' as it was the only café in Yarm at the time so no differentiation was needed. To complicate things slightly, there was a shop called Danby's on the opposite side of the High Street which was known locally as an ice-cream parlour even though it sold coffee and had a café. The logic of the townsfolk of Yarm in the 1960s.

The Bests had a blond-haired son called Simon who was a youngster, like me. As we got older, his interest in the dividing door that linked our side to the other side on the second-floor landing became evident and unwanted, and all because it had a keyhole. Within my bedroom there was yet another dividing door, with another keyhole, which in an ideal world would have been a door to Narnia but, as luck would have it, the door led straight onto *their* second-floor landing. The door was permanently locked on our side like the others, but it was a door I came to fear and any feeling of safety and security in my bedroom vanished.

Dad ran a 'VG' grocer's shop on the ground floor with a vast warehouse behind the shop and another one up above it, behind our back kitchen. I was not sure what 'VG' actually meant but told my friends it meant 'Very Good'. Not because I was *bad to the bone* and lying but because it sounded like a friendly kind of shop to live above.

Our living quarters were on the first floor and comprised a kitchen, a lounge and a separate dining room. The second floor had three bedrooms and a bathroom and it was an enormous place to call home. Every room on our side of the house was huge, high and horrifically cold. In winter, Jack

Frost visited day after day, carving feathered patterns of ice on the inside of every window, upstairs and down, and chilblains swelled our heels for months, racking them with pain. My favourite room was the kitchen, the hub of our home, which offered respite from the cold with the welcoming warmth of the coke-fired Aga. Every week, a huge ham roasted all night in a steel ham press, ready to sell in the shop the next day. The delicious aroma wafted through every room and if Dad and I tried to pinch even a sliver, a voice would pipe up from the distance somewhere, pointing out sternly, 'It's no good eating our profits, Sandy.'

We never worked out how she knew what we were doing, but Dad and I still managed to sneak some on the odd occasion, sharing a secret grin as it melted in our mouths.

Thank goodness for my dad, who had a wicked sense of humour and an air of mischief about him, just like me. At least he made life bearable in our house, although most of his days were spent in the shop and we had little precious time together.

Sundays in our house were the exception and only spoiled by the torture that was Sunday lunch. After our singsong in the local chapel, I skipped back home along the High Street at Dad's side, to see Mum in full flight, preparing lunch. The two of us would retire to the dining room and listen to his favourite songs from various Gilbert and Sullivan musicals. Then the command would come, telling us lunch was ready. We both knew it was best to obey immediately.

'Lunch is ready. *Now*, or it'll get cold.'

Mum had this obsession that food must be piping hot and it was like shoving a gas poker into my mouth, burning my throat as I swallowed. Sunday lunch, as it was called in our house, took place in the kitchen, as the dining room was reserved for Christmas and Easter family 'get-togethers' and Mum's highfalutin cocktail parties. Dinner took place in the evenings because, after all, this was an aspiring middle-class home. Mum was furious with me if I got the two words the wrong way round and her tight-lipped look would correct me. 'The Look' would tell me how stupid I was.

What does it matter? I used to think to myself. *Lunch ... Dinner ... they're only words and we all know what we mean.*

Anyhow, Sundays saw the three of us sitting down for lunch surrounded by static crackling from the old brown wireless on top of the sideboard, and not a morsel passed our lips until we closed our eyes and put our hands together, to thank the Lord and say grace.

There were never many conversations between us, simply Mum's beady eye monitoring me to make sure I was eating correctly and sitting up straight like a perfect princess. One Sunday, she screamed at me for saying the word 'burp'. Now, this was not because I had dared to say a word like that. It was just the wrong word to use. It was a brand-new word I had learned at school, along with how to fake a burp, and I had been practising in my bedroom.

Letting out the biggest burp and surprising even myself, I knew I had gone too far and rushed to apologise, feeling the panic setting in, saying, 'Pardon me. I burped. I'm sorry ... I'm so sorry.'

Dad stifled a grin, as Mum slammed her knife and fork down on the table with the words,

'How dare you? Common people say 'burp', Anne. We are *not* common in this house, and we say 'belch'. Get down from the table immediately and go to your room.'

Mum's eyes narrowed and a hefty clout stung my thigh as I climbed down from my chair, appalled at my own behaviour.

I was only being silly, I thought, as I sat staring out onto the High Street below wondering if my real mum would have told me off for the fake burp incident. I knew she would not. These were fleeting thoughts at first, but they were in the back of my mind, simmering, festering and then emerging every time I was in trouble and growing stronger with each passing year. I obsessively fabricated the perfect persona of my real mum and prayed at night that one day the 'Mum' I had would be proud of me, for some reason. Any reason would do. I just needed love and to be allowed to be a child. I also needed to be allowed a smidgeon of mischief from time to time.

I hated Sunday lunchtimes with a passion. Roast beef made me gag in a horrid kind of way that I couldn't control, and I felt sick even before Mum served it up, knowing what was to come. I also hated soggy, overcooked vegetables, and so Sunday lunch was quite a long affair with us all having to stay at the table, Mum glaring at me until that last mouthful disappeared from my plate.

It was torture, until at the age of eight I learned 'The Hamster Trick'. I swallowed as much as I could and then squirrelled away the rest into the sides of my cheeks as the *BBC Light Programme* spouted forth with *Family Favourites*. Intermittent conversations between Mum and Dad about the songs on the radio took the focus away from me and my cheeks stashed full of food. As soon as Mum started to clear away, I would excuse myself saying I needed to go to the toilet – where I slowly spat my stash down the pan. Now all I had to suffer was a stodgy dessert and Sunday lunch would be over for another week.

No matter what day it was, I had to ask for permission to get down from the table.

'Can I get down please, I'm full?'

'Wrong,' said 'The Look'.

According to Mum, the word 'can' meant you were physically able to get down from the table, 'may' was the right word when seeking permission, and 'I'm full' was simply rude. 'The Look' would tell me I must try again. How was I supposed to remember all this when I did not understand?

'You know fine well, Anne, it's please *may* I get down, I've had *sufficient.*'

A hefty clout stung my thigh each time I got it wrong and Mum justified this by adding,

'That'll teach you to remember next time.'

I started to practise getting the words, 'can', 'may' and 'sufficient' ready for the appropriate time, but it always came out wrong and I ended up with yet another raised palm mark reddening my young skin.

On another Sunday, I asked the unthinkable. From the smell wafting out of the Aga, I worked out we were having roast chicken for lunch instead of beef. That was a bonus for me, and I piped up with my request,

'Mum, do you think we could have Yorkshire puddings today with the roast chicken?'

She swung round to face me and sighed, saying, 'Of course not, you *stupid girl*. People only have Yorkshire puddings with beef. Everyone knows that!'

Why can't you have them with roast chicken? I wanted to ask, but I stayed silent. Her mind was made up.

I never understood the reason, and still do not to this day, but nowadays I eat Yorkshire puddings with roast chicken and thoroughly enjoy the naughtiness of the whole situation.

On Sunday afternoons, the fireplace in the lounge was lit up by a blazing coal fire, offering some warmth to Dad and me as we watched a cowboy film or a war film and were just happy to be together. Mum hardly ever joined us – preferring to do the ironing in the back kitchen.

If Dad tried to persuade her to join us, she would say, 'I couldn't *think* of ironing in the lounge, Sandy, especially on a Sunday.'

For most of the film, I stood behind his armchair as he relaxed on his day off from the shop, combing and styling his Brylcreemed hair into thin grey plaits all over the top of his head. He looked so funny, and he didn't mind one bit. An air of peace and happiness floated around us on those Sunday afternoons without Mum, amid the bloody battles happening on the screen. I loved being with my dad and felt so close to him. Periodically, he would scold Sooty the cat for extreme flatulence as she sat curled up on the rug by the fire, and it was only one Sunday when I noticed that Sooty was nowhere to be seen, that I understood the joke.

After a while, Mum would appear and shout at me, telling me to leave my dad's hair alone and give him some peace, adding every time, 'You look ridiculous, Sandy! I don't know why on earth you let her do it.'

It was ironic really that I was reprimanded, because the sentence that followed ended Dad's peace anyway.

'Right, time for our walk.'

I quickly learned that it was best to do as my dad did, and that was to do as Mum said – then it would be a pleasant Sunday for everyone. I know Mum was probably doing her best to keep my dad's heart as fit as anyone could, but seeing him stop, time after time – to get his breath back as we climbed up The Spital bank on our walk, brought tears to my eyes, and I wanted to shout at her for being so cruel. The three of us would stand in silence with Dad's chest heaving as he leaned on his walking stick, and Mum impatiently waiting to continue. The Spital was about three hundred yards to the left of our shop, at the end of the High Street, and I often wondered why we couldn't turn right as we set off so that Dad could enjoy a flat walk round the river banks without struggling each time. The Sunday walk continued for as long as I can remember and each time Dad tried his best to carry on. I truly loved him and often wondered why Mum had to push him to his limit, but at that age I think you believe all grown-ups are immortal, and I would never have dared question her judgement. It was such a shame that, in all those years, we never turned right. Poor Dad.

Sunday night was bath time so that I could start the school week with my hair and body freshly washed. Over the years, it also became 'Question Time': questions blunt, to the point and formed in the only way I knew how to ask them. As I sat there in the three inches of lukewarm water with my teeth chattering, the questions poured out while Mum washed me and scrubbed my neck to within an inch of its life.

The only question I desperately needed her to answer was asked only twice because 'The Look' told me I had almost crossed the line of impertinence.

'Why was I adopted?'

'I'll tell you when you're older and can understand.'

I was not about to give up and, summoning all my courage, I crossed the line. I tried again using different words,

'Why didn't my real mum want me?'

'I don't know, Anne, but we do. Now let's get that neck washed.'

And that would be it. I felt as if I was in big trouble for asking and that the word 'adopted' was like a swear word to her. Mum answered my questions in such a way as to close the subject for that particular bath time, and I dared not continue. I still remember the way her back would straighten and her mouth would set in a firm smile as she answered with as few words as possible. She probably dreaded Sunday night bath time. Even though her answers shut me up for a while, I couldn't understand why I was so different from her and why I was constantly on edge in her strait-laced company.

After Sunday night bath times, I lay in bed wondering who I was and making up stories in my head about why my real mum didn't want me and why *this* mum did not love me. I concluded each time that one thing was a fact and that thought stayed with me as I drifted off to sleep with sadness in my heart … *I'm not good enough to love … I'm not good enough to love …*

Somewhere deep inside I already knew that I was an 'imperfect fit' for the Mum who was destined to raise me. I wasn't like her at all. I didn't look like her, and I was terrified of her if the truth was known. At that young age, I already knew I would never become the 'pink-kind-of-girl' she had pictured when she adopted me. As if to emphasise her desire, my second-floor bedroom overlooking the High Street was utterly pink, including the skirting boards and ceiling, and remained steadfastly so for all the years I lived there.

Every day without fail, that familiar smack stung my thigh and I delved deep into my young mind, trying to work out what I had done to anger her. I would stare at the red palm print rising from my skin and wonder why she didn't like me. I tried so hard to be good, but the smacks kept on coming and soon made me believe I was, in fact, a bad girl. Quickly, I learned to hold back the tears as the pain overtook me, pressing my lips together and silently shouting to myself, 'Don't cry,' but that did not help. It made her angry that I did not crumble in front of her and another smack would land, for good measure. Then, for the rest of the day, she would ignore me completely which left me trying to work out how to please her and gain her love. That feeling of wanting to please others to gain affection has stayed with me all my life.

She also created an atmosphere of tension and anxiety in me that has never gone away. My fear of her taught me to constantly watch for signals in her facial expressions to try and avoid the daily smacking and I learned to keep my distance from her.

Our household was laden with authoritarian rules and uncompromising routines, all governed by Mum. At dinnertimes, Dad and I knew exactly what to expect on our plate, depending on the day, as the menu remained the same, week after week, month after month, year after year, except for Tuesdays – for some reason. I looked forward to some days and dreaded others, waking up each morning and working out what would be for dinner that day because I knew every last mouthful had to go before I could ask, 'Please *may* I get down, I've had *sufficient*?'

Tuesday's dinner was a surprise but the dreaded rice pudding that followed, topped with burnt skin, was discussed many a time by Dad and me. If we caught Mum in a good mood, which wasn't very often, we reminded her that neither of us liked rice pudding. We were continually amazed by the surprise on her face and the promise to make something different the following Tuesday. She never did.

I looked forward to Saturdays, as I knew bacon, egg, sausages and fried bread would be on the menu. It was a treat for Dad because, with his diagnosis of angina at the age of forty-two, fried food was allowed once a week, maximum. Mum's orders. Goodness knows what the spotted dick puddings, the treacle tarts and the bread-and-butter puddings swimming in a huge pool of lumpy custard did to my dad's heart, but Mum liked her puddings, or shall we say desserts?

According to Mum, there was no such thing as a pudding. All things eaten after dinner were called a dessert, but woe betide anyone who called the spotted dick or the bread-and-butter pudding a dessert. I understood none of the differentiation between the two words, so I chose to obliterate both from my vocabulary as I was terrified of making another mistake and seeing 'The Look' glare at me before the slap landed.

When I look back without fear involved, Mum's culinary routine was comforting in a way. It was a familiar routine. I knew what to expect and the exact day to expect it. Apart from Tuesdays, of course.

Around the age of nine, I became interested in learning to cook and suggested I could try making dinner once a week but was turned down flat.

'You take so long to do anything, Anne, we'll all be past it. And you're bound to get it wrong. It's much easier to do it myself.' I never asked again but wondered why her answers to me were always negative.

It was always 'No'.

I also wondered why she added the word 'Anne' whenever she spoke to me, and why the tone of her voice always made me feel so small. She instilled a tightness in me that I have carried through life, making me on edge and wary of conversations, in case I say the wrong thing, to anyone.

Just for a while now, I would like to stop thinking about how Mum constantly made my shoulders lift with trepidation and fear and introduce both the High Street I grew up in and the establishments which were part of my everyday life, as well the people I knew back then who were to influence my childhood.

In the '50s and '60s, Yarm was a sleepy town that saw little traffic passing through. It was a town of proud individual shopkeepers selling all the necessities and everyone knew each other so well.

Across the High Street from our shop and towards the old stone bridge, was the Silver Hairpin hairdressers. Bustling with smart middle-aged ladies all having their shampoo and set ready for the weekend, along with well-to-do ladies treating themselves to a fashionable blue rinse. You would never spot Mum in there as she preferred to do her own hair. Each night, she stood in front of the bathroom mirror, curling and twirling individual strands of dampened hair and, taking two hairgrips at a time that she had perfectly positioned between her teeth, she put them across each curled strand, in the shape of crosses all over her head. This was the way she slept and it ensured that she had pristine wavy hair by the morning. A hairnet completed the picture and I often wondered what Dad made of it all.

Moving along the High Street, Chadwick's sweet shop was a must. On the rare occasions I was allowed to visit, my taste buds were raring to go and my little legs had to negotiate the deep concrete step, my mouth salivating at the thought of what was on offer inside. Upon opening the door, the bell tinkled happily to let Mrs Chadwick or her son know a customer was on their way in. Mrs Chadwick was a smiley old lady who wore a flowery cotton pinny. Her son occasionally helped her out and doubled up as the local scoutmaster on a Friday night. Together for six days a week, they sold the most delicious-tasting sweets, and the sugary smell when you walked through their door was tantalisingly powerful. Colourful confectionery in tall glass jars stood side by side like soldiers on rows of shelves around the walls of the shop, looking down at me and begging me to buy them. As a child, it was a magical place to wander into even though our shop sold sweets too. I watched in wonder as old Mrs Chadwick slowly carried her wobbly wooden ladder from the back of the shop, limping all the while, leaned it precariously against one of the shelves and climbed up it to reach my requested jar. Pineapple Chunks that pricked my tongue as I sucked off their sugar coating to reach the smoothness inside, Mint Humbugs that took my breath away and made my nostrils ache and Lemon Sherbets that made me wink with delight as I bit into the centre. The choice went on and on. They were all so tempting and tasted much better than any of the sweets in packets that we sold. Occasionally, as I got older and after my dad had sneaked some money into my hand for doing odd jobs, I would race across the High Street, bound up the step and stride into Chadwick's feeling like a queen,

'A quarter of Pineapple Chunks please, Mrs Chadwick.'

'Of course, Madam,' she would say with a grin.

This was a whole four ounces and enough to make you feel sick if you ate them all at once. Whatever I could afford, which was usually two ounces, she dropped into a small, square, white paper bag, deftly twirling the top corners over, to make sure none of the precious sweets fell out on my way home.

Just up the High Street from Chadwick's was Danby's ice-cream parlour. In later years it housed a dimly-lit coffee bar at the back of the shop, hidden away from the eyes of the local adults and the place to be as a teenager. Next door was Aline's grocery shop where I became a traitor to our shop and got a Saturday job. Moving on, there was Dr Fraser's house where Anita, one of my friends, lived. Walking into Anita's hallway was like entering a palace; it had the most amazing mahogany banister, which scaled the full three floors of the house. What speed you could get up to when sliding down it was nobody's business – until, of course, we were found out and banned from it for ever.

Further down the High Street, past all the old cottages, was another shop called Robinson's, this time a hardware shop. It was like going into a treasure trove. Row upon row of worn, wooden shelves lined the shop, and hundreds of little wooden drawers full of weird and wonderful metal objects that I loved to look at, even though I didn't have a clue what most of them were. Warmed by a single heater, the shop smelled of paraffin and newly sawn wood from the kindling stacked by the door. Walking towards the key-cutting machine at the back, a metallic smell mixed with oil hit me every time. Mr and Mrs Robinson were kindly folk who allowed me to drift about investigating the contents of the wooden drawers, knowing that I would have no earthly use for any of their wares apart from taking home the items on Dad's special list. I would pick up objects that fascinated me from the drawers and take them to Mr Robinson who, with profound patience, helped me to learn the difference between such things as a screw, a nail, a nut and a bolt. He let me try finding the things on Dad's list before offering his help, and month by month my knowledge grew. They had no children of their own and they enjoyed me chattering away to them. In the school holidays, I would sit on the flagged floor by their heater, next to the key-cutting station, and pass the time of day with them; a mug of warm, milky tea cupped in my hand as I watched and learned as customers bought their goods. After each visit, I used to lie in bed wondering if I was related to the Robinson's because I couldn't work out why visiting their shop was so precious to me.

Just before the stone bridge and on the other side of the High Street, stood the surgery of the dreaded Dr Griffiths, whose bedside manner was non-existent. He was a portly, poker-faced doctor with a booming voice, and he seemed to hate children. I remember being treated for ringworm there and he hinted to Mum that I was neglected for having contracted it. She was told to keep me away from our pets and look after them properly. Mum raised herself to her full height and retorted that I had more than likely caught it on a customer's farm, that our pets had no disease, and she would be pleased if he didn't use that tone of voice to her again. Dr Griffiths silently took it all in with a blank stare. *So I must have some kind of disease,* I thought, as I sat there, petrified. *What is ringworm anyway?*

Is it because I'm adopted? Am I going to die? All sorts of questions whizzed through my head. I was brought back to reality when Dr Griffiths instructed me to strip down to my knickers and get up on the wooden chair next to him.

'Stand still, Anne. This could hurt,' was all he said, and he sprayed my whirly red ringworm spots with cold ether. Oh, the agony. I bit my lip to stop myself from screaming each time the freezing cold spray battered my body. I soon worked out I might not die because Dr Griffiths must have thought I was worth treating, or maybe he just revelled in seeing his patients writhing about in pain. After that, I never openly admitted to feeling poorly, knowing that Mum would haul me back down the High Street to the surgery of the dreaded Dr Griffiths.

In the years that followed, I contracted German measles and could not hide the rash from Mum, so she took me to Dr Fraser's surgery instead (the dad of my friend 'Anita with the banister') and he became our family doctor. Was this because Mum knew Dr Fraser would never speak to her as Dr Griffiths had done? Possibly it was because she liked to hear him remark in amazement, each time we saw him,

'I can't believe how much Anne looks like you.' Then he paused and added, 'considering she's adopted.' *How does Doctor Fraser know*? I always wondered.

Along from Dr Griffiths' surgery stood Hedley's Auctioneers. Mr Hedley was a red-faced, larger-than-life auctioneer, who always wore a deerstalker hat, a tweed jacket and checked tweed plus fours. He reminded me of Sherlock Holmes and whenever he came into our shop, I couldn't stop staring at him, thinking how brave he was to wear clothes that were so unusual. Mum always dressed me in clothes that were prim and proper. I somehow knew that my real mum would have turned heads in the way that she dressed, just like Mr Hedley did. Heading further along towards our shop was the Post Office with its red pillar box and two red telephone boxes outside on the footpath. Both telephone boxes were ingrained with the stench of cigarettes and had puddles of stale urine in the corners, but that did not prevent my best friend Pauline and me racing down there after dinner one night, at twelve years old, to ring a boy from school called Paul.

♫♫ *We love you, yeah, yeah, yeah* ♫♫

As soon as he answered, we shoved a twopenny bit into the coin receptacle, giggling like crazy, and pledged our undying love to him by singing The Beatles song 'She Loves You' down the lines but changing the lyrics to 'We love you, yeah, yeah, yeah.' He didn't say a word and, not knowing what to do next, we hung up. The following day at school he ignored us both and we knew our love was not meant to be.

Along from the Post Office, there is still an old marble plaque on the front wall of The George and Dragon pub, commemorating a moment of fame in my hometown of Yarm.

Stockton and Darlington railway plaque of 1820.

Next door is another pub, the Union Arms, which doubled up as a hotel and, while they were on stage in Stockton-on-Tees, all the famous people stayed there. As a young girl, I used to fly along the pavement on my roller skates to ask wide-eyed and politely for their autographs, all of which I treasured and kept in a brown fake-leather autograph book for years and years. Flipping through it every week in my room brought back their faces and my shy conversations with them and I was amazed at having met some famous actors. They included David Kossoff, John Alderton, and all the cast from the '60s police drama, Z Cars. However, my favourite autograph of all time was my dad's which said, 'To Dad's second sweetheart.' I still have that tattered autograph book as a reminder of his love for me.

Walking a little further, Spark's bakery shop sold scrumptious strawberry tarts topped with swirly piped cream, which on rare occasions I ate whilst wandering off the High Street, down Chapel Wynd, to the Methodist Chapel by the river, where I went with my dad each Sunday to have a right good sing-song. Built by John Wesley, it is the oldest octagonal chapel in the world. The entrance to the chapel became a 'special place' as a teenager, with Bert, the first love of my life. God should have struck us down on the spot for what we got up to there.

Back on the High Street, stood a posh double-fronted shop called Strickland and Holt which began life as a high-class chemist run by Mr Holt himself. Now known simply as Stricki's, it is not only a place to buy expensive clothes and collectibles but also a place to be seen having one of the twelve types of coffee on offer at an exorbitant price. They produce a salad dressing, simply called 'Yarm Salad Dressing', which is sold internationally and I can understand why. It's the 'little bit of love' listed in the ingredients which sets it apart from any other salad dressing. Or maybe I'm biased because it is made in Yarm.

Next door was the Black Bull Inn and upstairs was their function room where, in 1967, Mum and Dad celebrated twenty-five years of Mum laying down the law, and Dad adhering to it. The owners, Mr and Mrs Carr, laid on a beautiful spread for them, including a whole baked salmon adorning the centre of a groaning buffet table. At the time, buffets were all the rage and a brand new way to eat. A self-service sort of way, and the guests were excited to be queuing to help themselves to the amount of food seen as polite. For the first time, at thirteen years old, Mum allowed me to wear a 'bit-of-a-mini-dress'. A pale-pink crocheted shift dress with a Peter Pan collar and two huge square, mother-of-pearl buttons diverting attention away from my continuously sprouting breasts.

The last pub before ending up at our shop again was The Green Tree, run by Mr and Mrs Beckwith. Another friend, Christine, lived there above the pub, and we were inseparable. She was three years older than me and she was my heroine. We walked hand in hand on many an adventure around the nearby streets of Yarm, to play with children of other shop owners. She was so pretty and kind and even when she locked me in the understairs cigarette cupboard of their pub during a game of hide-and-seek, I was not frightened because I trusted her completely. I knew it was just a game and huddled in the corner in the pitch-black waiting for my release. Unfortunately, she kept me in there so long that a search party – consisting of Mum and Dad – scoured the streets of Yarm looking for me. When they eventually singled out the pub as another possibility, Christine denied all knowledge of my whereabouts. Her big, brown eyes full of innocence must have fooled my parents as they left the Beckwith's pub empty-handed.

In later years, she told me that her only reason for lying was that she wanted me to stay and play with her. How naughty was that!

You will have worked out by now that my freedom was curtailed for a while and another red wheal appeared on my legs before I was sent to bed without any dinner.

'She locked me in,' I could have cried but remained silent, taking the punishment without argument. I knew Mum would not believe me.

Christine, my 'big' friend, her brother, Stephen and myself
venturing further afield to pick flowers
(photo courtesy of Christine).

Yarm also had a vinegar brewery on the banks of the river, just over the old stone bridge, and a tannery close by it. A fellmonger too, which happened to be right behind our shop. It employed hundreds of locals and the work involved the curing and drying of sheep pelts and sheep's wool. The factory gave off a putrid smell caused by decaying fat and meat which still clung to the pelts before the curing process began, along with the smell of the chemicals used in this treatment. It enveloped the whole of the High Street if the wind was blowing in the wrong direction, and on those occasions, every room in our house reeked of it and almost took my breath away. On top of this, the factory pumped a foamy, green effluent through underground pipes straight into the River Tees behind our shop. Made up of a mixture of lime and sulphuric acid, it completely contaminated the river for miles with the visible effluent travelling upstream or downstream, depending on the direction of the tide. The 'Skinyard smell', however, was 'normal' to us and we all accepted it as part of our lives growing up there.

Since those days in the '50s and '60s, Yarm has changed dramatically. The factories are long gone, and an overload of extortionately priced housing estates has exploded in the surrounding area. Nowadays, the town exudes money with its overpriced shops littering the High Street, expensive restaurants and cafes, including of course the ubiquitous Costa Coffee. I swear I'm right in thinking that in the next few years no one will have any free hands for anything practical, as they continue to carry their mobile in one hand and their new-fangled appendage of a takeaway coffee in the other.

The number of absolutely enormous four-wheel-drive cars and out-of-this-world top-end cars is so high, yet only a handful of their drivers can manoeuvre them properly in and out of the small, crowded parking bays on the cobbled High Street. Each day is a constant shuffle of vehicles wanting to come off the cobbles into the main flow of traffic, and courtesy seems to be a thing of the past. Chaos rules, as other vehicles drive slowly along the High Street, trying to spot a vacant parking bay; delivery vans and articulated lorries are unloading on the side of the road, blocking in parked vehicles, and local buses are stopping to allow passengers to embark or disembark. Add to that the fact that all through traffic has to pass through Yarm High Street to reach any destination at all, north or south, and the phrase 'snail's pace' springs to mind. Watching all this conjures up the memory for me of the peaceful bygone days in the '50s and '60s, growing up there with little traffic.

Yet there is still something utterly magical about the place and, no matter how it changes, Yarm-on-Tees is a place embedded in my heart.

My earliest recollection of being by myself in the High Street is of walking to nursery at the tender age of three-and-a-half years old. Trotting along, towards the old stone bridge at the far end, without anyone beside me. How grown-up was I? How early my independent streak had reared its head.

A month after me starting nursery, Dad fell ill, and Mum had to work in our shop full-time. Three mornings a week, she set me across the High Street to undertake this exciting adventure. Looking back as I trotted along, I could see her standing at the door of our shop until she saw Miss Burton, my nursery teacher, come out to take me into her fold. I liked Miss Burton because she was called Burton, like me, and that felt warm. She was happy and kind and I wanted her to be my mum instead of the stony-faced Mum who had chosen me.

At the end of each morning, Miss Burton would keep me back until everyone else had been collected and then set me off back down the High Street towards home. I followed instructions to go to Olwyn's Wool Shop, opposite our shop, and Olwyn herself would see me across the road, back to safety.

Walking to nursery alone was the second time my independent streak had reared its head. The first time was planned by me, and me alone, and was impulsive through and through.

I cannot remember this event and only rely on what I have been told by Mum, Dad and Uncle Archer, who saved me.

Before we moved into the shop full-time, Mum and Dad still owned a house which they were in the process of selling, in a residential area called Eaglescliffe, about a mile north of Yarm. It was on the main road from Yarm to Stockton on Tees and stands there today, almost unchanged.

Apparently, Mum had strapped me into my pram in the front garden for some fresh air and gone back inside. Soon after, my Uncle Archer was hammering on the front door hand in hand with me and yelling Mum's name. Driving to Yarm, he'd spotted 'Blondie', as he called me, walking along with one foot on the pavement and one foot in the gutter (a sign of the times to come?), oblivious to the world. My trek towards Yarm took place when I was under three years old, and that independence and determination – some may call it stubbornness – has stayed with me all my life.

As a young child, it didn't take me long to work out that I was on life's journey alone. I felt different from other children even though my understanding of the whole adoption thing was limited. It was just words delivered to me by Mum and Dad, 'We adopted you.'

On other occasions it was something I heard in passing as people whispered to each other, their hands shielding their mouths, 'She's adopted you know.'

Grown-ups would monitor me intently as if I would suddenly sprout horns or my head would revolve like the girl in *The Exorcist* movie.

I wondered why Mum had to add the word 'adopted' every time she introduced me to someone, saying, '… and this is Anne, our adopted daughter.'

Why is it mentioned at all? I thought. *She told me to keep it a secret, didn't she?* Eventually, I worked out that mentioning the word 'adopted' took away the blame from Mum if I behaved badly, which I hardly ever did.

From an early age, I backed off from being introduced to anyone and stood with my head down, hoping to fade into the background. Mum's way of adding the word 'adopted' instilled in me that I was not good enough to be introduced simply as her daughter. The word surrounded me everywhere I went and, as my understanding grew, question after question festered within me.

Being adopted affected me more as each year passed and a yawning chasm between Mum and I made life worse. I had no one to go to for answers and no one to talk to about my thoughts. Okay, I had 'Question Time' during Sunday bath times, but the answers merely skated over the surface. I adored my dad and longed to approach him but I knew he had worries enough of his own.

Still, looking on the bright side, I was lucky to have a place like Yarm to grow up in and lucky to have my dad.

Maybe Yarm is so special to me because the High Street is where I learned to ride my squeaky blue second-hand bike at the age of six. I pedalled up and down the whole length, day after day with increasing speed and confidence. The feeling of freedom a bike gave me was wonderful, and I felt alive and carefree yet safe in the bosom of Yarm. I would ride along the pavements greeting all the familiar folk who knew me as The Burtons' 'adopted' daughter.

As I grew more daring and adventurous, the things I thought would naturally be allowed never were, and so the mischief began. Things like riding a little further away from home, without permission. Leaving the High Street and racing around the corner to West Street was something I couldn't resist. To stand underneath the enormous brick viaduct and feel the throbbing vibration of the steam trains as they rumbled overhead, enthralled and excited me. When the word got back to Mum via the wider community of Yarm, I was in big trouble. Dad felt the need to support Mum and made me promise never to go to West Street again. Then followed the inevitable smack on the legs, along with her stony-faced expression which lasted the rest of the day. 'And withdrawal of love?' I hear you ask. Yes, in bucketloads!

'I'm so disappointed in you, Anne. What will everyone think of us?'

This perfect little girl had made her second big mistake out in the big wide world, for all to see. The disappointment in Mum's eyes told the whole story. I couldn't understand what the big deal was. After all, I stayed on the pavement following her instructions to the letter. In my eyes, everyone who saw me would think *'there goes Anne Burton (adopted)'*, and they would have got on with their day. I knew I was safe. I knew everyone in Yarm and they knew me and my squeaky old bike. The only people who came to Yarm from the outside world were shoppers and the majority of them were customers of ours, so I knew them too.

Thinking back, there was one outsider who could have caused worry in a grown-up's head and that was Gigi, the tramp. Almost every day, he came on the service bus from Stockton and sat in the bus shelter underneath Yarm Town Hall. He was a sallow-faced, old tramp-of-a-man who always dressed in the same checked-brown long woollen coat and flat cap, and he stank like a skunk. Not that I had come across many skunks in Yarm High Street, but I imagined if I ever did then they would have smelt exactly like Gigi.

All the children in Yarm, including me, knew he wouldn't harm a fly. We enjoyed talking to him even though our parents forbade it. Occasionally we teased him and went too far until the tone of his voice changed and he started grunting and flailing his arms. This was a signal for us to quickly step back, avoiding the spit that sprayed out with his bellowing grunts. He hung around the bus shelter all day and then got on the bus to goodness knows where. Maybe he was homeless and the bus was a warm place to take shelter for a while before reaching Yarm. We felt sorry for Gigi and concocted various stories about his life as a tramp until one day he stopped coming and was never seen again. We assumed he had died. Poor Gigi. None of us ever found out if it was true.

One day while riding my bike up and down the High Street, I found a 'ten-bob' note lying there on the cobbles looking straight up at me. I was astonished at finding this huge amount of money. Believing the sensible thing to do was to hand it in, I pedalled like crazy across the cobbles and straight to the police station which was up High Church Wynd and back on the way to West Street. My bike and I got escorted home by the local bobby who explained to Mum, 'If it's not claimed in a fortnight, she can have it.'

My eyes lit up. How I longed for that fortnight to whizz by, knowing I would be rich and could at last fulfil the promise I made to myself many times in bed, of running away to Butlin's.

My dad was proud of me for being honest and using my initiative, but once again Mum was disappointed by my actions. She said I should have come home and been *told what to do* rather than making a decision by myself.

'You know that, Anne. Why do you always do the wrong thing? Anyway, how come you saw the money from the pavement in the first place? Just tell me that.'

I was sent to my room and worked something out that day – a way to win Mum's approval and maybe even a smidgeon of love. All I had to do was to stop thinking for myself and let her control me and then I might get a hug or a kind smile from her.

Be the perfect daughter, I told myself.

It was a lesson learned early in life, and that was the day I dug a trench and laid subconscious and deep foundations in the beginning of 'The Wall Against Mum'. After days like those, I lay awake in bed with tears pricking my eyes, wondering why whatever I did was not good enough and why she delighted in making me feel small, unloved and unwanted. I would consciously turn all thoughts to my dad and concentrate on how much I loved him and how kind he was, and sleep would come at last.

My dad was my saviour. To skip and jump beside him on a Sunday morning was a wonderful feeling as we made our way along the High Street towards the chapel. Skipping and jumping over 'The Bogeymen' on the pavements, and the occasional burst of speed to keep up with him, laughing all the while. He would take my tiny hand in his and remind me, 'We'll be in for a good sing-song this morning, Tish. You'll enjoy that.'

'I know I will, Tosh,' and squeezing his hand we would carry on walking down the wynd to Yarm Chapel.

I remember how special my nickname made me feel. I was his precious little girl and the rare times we had alone together were always fun. He used a special two-toned whistle only for me and whenever I heard it, I flew to his side. I knew his love for me would always be there and unless I did something very, very bad, he would never be disappointed in me. He was a man who hated confrontations, unlike Mum who seemed to relish them. He was the peacekeeper.

My dad's voice was that of a true Methodist. Resonant, tuneful and extremely loud. I loved to stand beside him and crane my neck to watch him sing. Tosh and Tish would sing their hearts out and it was easy to forget that this gentle dad of mine was such a poorly man.

Sunday school anniversaries filled me with joy, as I stood in front of the heaving congregation in the pretty Wesleyan chapel, and sang like a 'little bird', according to my dad. We were proud to belong to each other. I knew I had another dad somewhere out there but I hardly ever tried to picture him. This dad, my dad, would do for me.

(*'This Little Bird' – Marianne Faithful – 1965*)

After being adopted, I became part of a family of upright and honest people who guided me as they saw fit. My dad guided me with love and affection and I knew he found it hard to understand Mum's words and actions towards me. She was strict and unfeeling and the thought of having fun with me never entered her head. I had been chosen by a 'children should be seen and not heard' kind of Mum, and she often said those words to me if I was being 'silly'. Looking back, I think she had to prove to all around her that she could mould me into perfection, to show that this adopted child was not *bad blood*. Such a harsh thing to expect of any child, and I lived with the control and her wish to have me as a perfect possession, rather than love me for who I was.

I became part of a wider family of wealthy Christian relations. I inherited five male cousins and one female who were all much older than me, and enormously tall.

There was a right way and a wrong way to do everything, from holding my knife and fork, to greeting my relations at Christmas. The right way was always Mum's way, and everything became more difficult for me to achieve as I grew older. I began to wonder why I was there at all. Mum continued to be one of the social climbers of Yarm, organising various events and striving to be the president of all the clubs around the town. I was just in the way.

I soon learned to become 'the listener' at all of our family gatherings in case I said or did the 'wrong thing'. There were times when I was allowed to go and join my male cousins in another room to play with their train sets and all other toys meant for boys. These were the best times I had as part of our extended family and way better than sitting at Mum's feet, listening to my relations nattering on and on and forgetting various people's names as they reported the highlights that had occurred since their last meeting.

As soon as my cousins and I reassembled with the family, Mum was poised, ready to pipe up with the phrase, 'Right … time for Anne's party piece,' no matter how hard I prayed that she would forget.

Clapping her hands to bring everyone to attention, she turned to me with an expression that said, 'Up you get.'

This was my cue to stand up in front of everyone and sing a song, with a smile on my face, or dance a dance, with a smile on my face, and keep the smile there all the while until my relations had finished clapping and saying how wonderful I was. *Still adopted though*, I could practically hear them thinking out loud. I felt anything but wonderful. I felt like hiding in a dark corner and hoping that another cousin would be chosen to perform but somehow the boys had their toys, and I was the shy showgirl. It never occurred to me to tell Mum and Dad how much I deplored being pushed into the limelight, but even if it had, I wouldn't have had the courage to do so and nothing would have altered anyway. It was a gruelling expectation that everyone automatically assumed I looked forward to. I hated being on show, knowing I had to perform perfectly or 'The Look' would return and stay there for the rest of the day. I soon learned to carry out my party piece with eyes avoiding Mum.

('Will Your Anchor Hold (in the Storms of Life)' – Priscilla Owens – hymn, circa 1849)

('Love Divine All Loves Excelling (Blaenwern)' – Charles Wesley – hymn, circa 1890)

5

Denied Emotions and My Music

From six years old, most conversations with Mum, or should I say most speeches since they were always one-sided, were about good ways to live your life and putting other people first.

'Do unto others as you would have them do unto you.'

'Think of others before yourself.'

I agree wholeheartedly that fulfilling both biblical proverbs is a fine way to live your life, but to be able to develop as a person must surely involve thinking of yourself too, at some point. Throughout my childhood, Mum reminded me that other people's happiness came first, and I must take the back seat and never show disappointment.

How about other emotions and being allowed to show them? Oh no, that would never do. Showing true emotions like happiness, excitement, anger, sadness, or any other emotion was not accepted by her. I was told it was wrong to show any emotion whatsoever, whether it be a positive or negative one.

'Be quiet, Anne. All this laughing never did anyone any good,' she would say when all I was doing was being happy or excited about something.

When I had hurt myself badly and couldn't stop the tears from welling up and spilling over, she would scream at me saying, 'Stop crying you stupid girl. You're not hurt!'

The day I flew head first over the handlebars of my tricycle, testing out how quickly my front brakes worked, and smashed my forehead and nose onto the concrete in our back yard was not enough to warrant a cuddle. Flying up to the kitchen in tears with blood running down my face I was told, 'It's your own fault for being so stupid. Why can't you just ride it like a little lady?' She tended to my wounds but there were no arms of comfort to rush to and no kisses to make me better.

As I grew older, I learned to hide my emotions or to show the emotion I thought fitted the bill for her. If a true emotion slipped through the net and it did not fit, I was sent to my room and could be there for hours before she gave in and invited me down again.

Most Tuesdays, after school, became my 'I feel free' times and I longed for them to come round. On Dad's half-day closing from the shop, mild mischief reared its ugly head when he took me fishing with him. Even the maggots did not put me off. Trotting along beside him over farm fields and down to rivers, I felt relaxed, happy and much loved. Relaxed enough to ask questions about the world, happy enough to run and skip and sing songs at the top of my young Methodist voice. I suppose some would call it happiness but as a child who was usually denied the chance to show my emotions, this was mischief to me and it felt good. 'Happy Talk' from South Pacific was our favourite song to 'holler' as we walked side by side.

One Tuesday afternoon, having reached double figures, I remember being in a quiet mood on one of our fishing trips and simply listening to pop songs on my transistor radio while my dad waded out into the middle of the river. Picking my spot on the grass near the riverbank, I laid on my side and propped myself up on my elbow, watching him with my heart full of love and looking at the blue skies around us. It was a precious moment in my life, being there, just the two of us and I felt as if I belonged. No arguments, no questions being shot at me and no defensive responses stuttering from my mouth. Best of all, no one was watching me or waiting to pounce on any imperfect action of mine.

An earlier photograph of Tosh and Tish together, when I was six years old.

I can still picture that blissful day, with the DJ on Radio 1 playing 'A Whiter Shade of Pale' by Procol Harum and me lying back on the grass wondering what a vestal virgin was, determined to look it up when I got home.

My dad never asked why I needed to listen to 'that rot'. He was much more like me. He remembered the names of my musical heroes, could pick out their songs on the radio and understood why they excited me and had me singing along as I listened to them.

Dad's world was powered by music too, and even though it was not my kind of music we listened to it on many occasions and sang along together.

He was part of an amateur dramatic group called the Stockton Stage Society and with that wonderful voice, he played many a lead role in operettas and musicals including The Mikado, Oklahoma! and South Pacific, singing his heart out as he did in chapel. Music helped him to forget his worries for a while and he developed my unending love of popular music and the fact that it can transport you to another plane with its beat, rhythm and lyrics.

From eleven years old, when Dad's health started to fail, Tuesday evenings took on a whole new meaning for me. It was my 'waiting for Dad to return safely from Stockton Stage Society' time.

With Mum out climbing her social ladder at the Women's Institute, I was left alone in that huge house trying to ignore the various creaks and groans that emerged in the solitary silence of a building constructed in 1760. To distract me from feeling frightened, I would turn up the volume on the television to mask the noises. Then every Tuesday, I sat with my legs curled up on the lounge window seat overlooking the High Street and entered the world of whichever adventure book I was reading at the time.

As the next few years passed and my vigil continued, I changed my reading habits and delved into the teenage world of the 'Jackie' magazine.

Waiting for the three beeps of Dad's car horn, I tried to work out what the 'teenage' words meant in the heartfelt letters sent to the 'Cathy and Claire' problem page. I wondered if *I* should write a letter so they could help me sort out my ever-worsening relationship with Mum but knew they would not be interested. Most issues of the magazine included a technicolour pull-out poster of 'long-haired louts' as Mum called them. As I dare not ask to stick them onto my pink-painted bedroom wall, they all lay in a treasured pile in the bottom drawer of my bedside table, waiting for me to pick them up and drool over them once more, while humming their songs as I tried to work out my place in the world.

Perched on the window seat on those Tuesday evenings meant that even with the volume of the television turned up, I could hear the alert as Dad sounded his car horn. Hearing it beep three times was a code between us and it let me know he was safely home. It was also a signal to fling my reading matter down on the coffee table, race down the two flights of stairs and through to the back of the shop. There I would meet him, stooped and grey-faced, as he walked through the door from the backyard. I understood my next move and it had to be done swiftly.

Clutching a cup of water filled from the sink next to the backyard door, I manoeuvred his pain-racked body through the shop and led him by the hand to the bottom step of the staircase which led back up to the first floor of our house. As Dad lay back almost panting, I gently loosened his tie and the top button of his shirt. Delving into the inside pocket of his sports jacket, I grabbed the metal tube containing his tablets, twisted the top off and told him to open his mouth.

Each week I reassured him as I pulled him up to a sitting position with the words, 'Here, Dad, you'll be alright in a minute, I promise.' Putting a little white heart tablet onto his tongue, I held the cup of water to his lips and sat there entwining my other hand in his, watching his every move in case he choked.

After a few minutes his breathing slowed and became steady, and he was ready to be helped up the stairs back to another sleepless night of worry.

Fifty-four years since his death , Dad's metal tablet tube still holds vivid memories of those terrifying Tuesday evenings on the bottom step at Yarm.

I imagined that this weekly routine would go on for the rest of my life as my treasured dad was immortal in my eyes. One Tuesday evening, after his return from singing in Stockton, he changed my views completely as he confided in me.

'I can't remember driving home tonight, pet. I don't even know how I got here … I must have had a blackout.' I asked no questions even though that word meant nothing to me, but from that day on after looking up the meaning in my Encyclopaedia Britannica, I knew that something was so very wrong with him, and he was not a well man.

Growing up, there was always music around me. It filled my world and, to this day, music both old and new still plays a huge part in my life. Pre-teenage years, I listened to Radio Caroline and Radio Luxembourg and I wonder if Mum ever knew why I suddenly elected to go to bed early each night after I was given the little black transistor radio for my tenth birthday present.

As soon as I had been tucked in (and yes, that was still happening at ten years old) and I heard her close the lounge door below, I would silently sneak my radio 'under the bedclothes' and listen to it for ages, always with one ear cocked in case she came and caught me red-handed. My radio diverted my thoughts away from being an 'imperfect fit' for a while and gave me peace.

I loved listening to the music Johnny Walker played, gagging in horror at the jokes Tony Blackburn told and even Jimmy Savile as he welcomed us all as part of his *Under the Bedclothes Club,* seemed friendly. Little did any of us pre-teens understand why he probably chose that name for his club in the first place.

Nowadays, Radio 2 is always on in the background, having graduated from Radio 1 many years ago. It was a big decision to move on, as it was an admission of age creeping up on me but made easier because some of my all-time favourite DJs had made the move before me and helped to pave the way.

I still watch Glastonbury each year and Jools Holland keeps me up to date with the new music on the scene. I joined Rod Stewart (my all-time musical hero) three years ago when he played at Newcastle Arena, and it nearly came to 'fisticuffs' as they say up there, when he 'wellied' a football out into the audience and it came flying my way. It bounced off the top of the empty seat right in front of me. I tried to catch it and it landed between my legs (only the football, alas) and from absolutely nowhere, a small bendy woman appeared at my knees and tried to snatch it away. I have never moved so fast for years and managed to grab it myself and hang on to it for dear life. It was signed by 'Rod the Mod' and it was mine, all mine. After all those years of seeing him kick footballs out into the audience at festivals, I was not going to let this one slip away.

The signed football now sits proudly in my home and even my dear granddaughters have access denied.

Footballs are for boys anyhow, aren't they?

('Happy Talk' – South Pacific – 1949)

('When My Little Girl Is Smiling' – Jimmy Justice – 1962)

('A Whiter Shade of Pale' – Procol Harum – 1967)

6

Calliper Days

Mum carted me off to Middlesbrough General Hospital when she spotted another chink in my armour. I had knock knees.

Not content with trying to mould me emotionally into being her perfect daughter, now it was time to tackle the physical side of me and make it just right, like the bear's chair in Goldilocks.

I was four years old, and the solution was a severe and lengthy process. I had to wear metal callipers day in and day out for just over a year. I already knew I was adopted and different in some way from the other boys and girls but having to wear callipers made me physically different as well. Now, everyone was bound to look at me and notice my two revolving heads along with legs that would not bend.

To Mum, this was a short period of hardship to perfect my legs, altering them into legs expected of a perfect daughter. I can vividly remember the day the doctor fitted those horrible, heavy callipers onto my little legs, and he pushed my feet into special clumpy, brown shoes, with holes in the side to fix each calliper in place. The metal braces rose up the sides of my legs to the top of my thighs. They had brown leather knee restraints and brown leather hoops around the top of my legs, and they hurt.

As soon as the doctor fitted them, he told me to get up and walk (his name was not Jesus by the way), and I immediately fell over and cracked my head on an old gas fire in his room. Once I had been made vertical, I left the hospital with singed hair as well as callipers. Not a good start.

I hoped Mum and Dad would take them off my legs at bedtime, but this was not to be, and so bedtime became even more of an invisible enemy. Going to bed before I had to wear those dreadful things had been uncomfortable anyway, due to Mum's tucking in routine. Each night, after making sure I was lying on my back, she tucked the bedclothes in so tightly around my feet and all the way along the side of the bed up to my chin, as if to say, 'Right then, you stay there until the morning … and don't move.'

I felt trapped and could not turn over. My big toes were bent under the taut sheet and the weight of the thick, heavy blankets on top of me. Untucking myself was not an option that crossed my mind at that young age, and I lay there immobilised until sleep slowly descended upon me.

At the age of seven, I plucked up the courage to mention how uncomfortable the tucking in felt and she replied, telling me it was a *proper nurses' bed corner technique* that she'd learned as a children's nurse in Liverpool, adding,

'Don't be silly, Anne. There's nothing wrong with the way I tuck you in. None of the children I looked after ever complained.'

Why Mum elected to become a children's nurse was beyond me as she did not seem to like children in the slightest.

Once the callipers came into play, I was tucked in as usual and clamped in metal too. My legs were weighted down and immovable and the only muscles moving were my eye muscles trying to stop the flow of tears.

One evening a few weeks later, Dad came up to the bathroom and heard my muffled sobs. When I told him what was wrong, he sat on the edge of the bed gently stroking my forehead and said, 'I'll have a word with Mum,' which meant Mum would make the final decision about the callipers coming off at bedtime. Dad must have fought so hard to reason with her, and I skipped around the kitchen the next night with a grin on my face after the callipers came off.

'If you're a good girl, we'll take them off at six o'clock each night, and you can go to bed without them,' Mum told me. I looked up at Dad and he winked at me, with a smile.

How quickly I learned to tell the time. Each evening, I watched the hands on the kitchen clock as they neared that magical hour, knowing I would be free. Bedtimes became comparative bliss and even the tucking in routine was easier to endure.

Trying to walk unaided took weeks of gritting my teeth and many a tumble along the way. It was impossible to get on and off a chair by myself at first, so what little independence I had enjoyed disappeared completely. But I was determined and, when there was no one about, I hauled myself up the mountain. The feeling of success and pride that overcame me as I finally made it to the top and sat down on the kitchen chair, complete with my callipers, was immeasurable. I tipped my head back and giggled to myself as I realised from that moment on, I could succeed in anything.

I devised ingenious ways of getting up the many flights of stairs in our huge *house above the shop*. By hanging on to the handrail and heaving myself up one stair at a time, legs splayed from the hips down, I managed to reach the bedrooms on the second floor. Going down was much easier and I saw it as fun. I simply sat on my bottom and slowly bounced down each stair until I reached the final stair of that flight. Then I would haul myself up to a standing position and carry on. When no one was watching, the handrail turned into my helper. As I became more adept, I flung one leg over it, carefully perfecting my balance between the two heavy leg irons and allowed my hands to guide me slowly one by one down the handrail, to the bottom. That was even more fun – and extremely dangerous, I suppose. I would have been in big trouble if I had been caught.

After Mum decided that callipers were necessary for her tiny imperfect daughter, the way she dressed me altered when Dad suggested that I should be allowed to wear trousers.

'No, she'll look like a boy,' was her initial response, but Dad insisted. From then on, frilly, frothy dresses hung unused in my pink wardrobe and trousers were the order of the day. Not just any trousers either; they were tartan trousers. Proper Scottish tartan trousers. I adored them, felt at home in them and it started my love of all things Scottish. Mum continued to adorn my hair with slides and bows but the tartan trousers saved the day and masked my physical difference throughout my calliper days.

Eventually, I learned to haul myself up onto one of the dining room chairs too and often sat alone studying the photo on the tattered sleeve of a regularly played single in my dad's record collection. Kenneth McKellar, a kindly-looking man in traditional Scottish dress smiled at me from the sleeve and the affinity between us grew the more Dad played his song. I adored his voice, the unmistakable accent, and was astounded that he, as a man, wore a kilt. The best thing was bordering on mischief and singing the word 'tac' at the top of my voice with Dad as Kenneth told us we could 'tac' the high road and he would 'tac' the low road – but added that he would still be in Scotland before us.

'Where is Scotland?' I asked my dad one Sunday, and he explained about the mountains, the lochs and the fact that it was another country above ours that people referred to as 'Bonny Scotland'. I made up my mind that when I grew up, I would go to Loch Lomond. Dad taught me the lyrics of the chorus and, trying our best to put on a full Scottish accent, we sang it time after time, laughing together at our mistakes.

As I got older, I somehow persuaded Mum to dress me in kilts as an alternative to the frothy dresses. Even though I did not really understand where Scotland was, I believed it was in my blood.

(*'Loch Lomond' – Kenneth McKellar – 1955*)

(*'Living Doll' – Cliff Richard and The Shadows – 1959*)

7

Cleveland School

Life at the 'big school' began in my fifth year after the doctor deemed that those metal monstrosities were no longer necessary. My legs were proclaimed perfect, or as perfect as they could ever be. Just like my older male cousins, I was put into the private education system. I longed to go to the local primary school in Yarm – on the way to West Street – but Mum had made her mind up. There were all the 'Mrs Joneses' of the neighbourhood for Mum to keep up with and sending me to Cleveland School meant that I would be mixing with all the Joneses' children and keeping up with them too. I wore a dark brown uniform with gold lettering adorning my blazer badge, unlike the pupils at Yarm Primary school who wore their everyday clothes.

To send me to Cleveland School must have cost my parents a fortune and a few troubled discussions, no doubt, about how to find the fees for the following term. I often wonder if going to Yarm Primary would have eased my dad's financial worries and helped his troubled heart. Maybe he would have been with me for longer in my life, but I will never know.

Cleveland School was at the far end of *The Avenue* in Eaglescliffe and about two miles north of Yarm, on the way to Stockton-on-Tees. *The Avenue* was a leafy residential lane, lined with enormous Victorian houses and gnarled old conker trees. The lane seemed to stretch to eternity until it reached a dead end, where the impressive school gates stood with a stone lion sat proudly on the top of each of the two weathered stone gateposts. The school building was magnificent but a little run down by the time my school years started. Various classrooms on the top floor had buckets positioned here and there, to collect the rainwater dripping through the leaky roof. The outside was fabulous. There were acres of grassy areas and wooded grounds belonging to the school. We were allowed to play freely in some areas and others were expressly forbidden. There was a special bank called 'Grassy Bank' where we enjoyed doing roly-poly's, learning to take turns so that we didn't collide with each other.

One day in my first year there, while waiting for my roly-poly turn, I was accosted by Jeremy Pace, a boy in my class, who planted a big kiss full on my lips and then ran hell for leather away from me. All the other children in the roly-poly queue burst out laughing and my face began to burn, but I didn't understand why.

When I got home that day it was the first thing I told Mum as I sat in the kitchen drinking my orange squash.

'Jeremy Pace kissed me today.'

She marched over to me and demanded to know the details, 'Where? Where did he kiss you, Anne?' Of course, she meant which part of my body had the kiss been planted on, but I didn't understand the question. I looked at her and whispered, 'On Grassy Bank.'

'You insolent child. Go to your room and stay there until I tell you to come down,' and the smack that followed almost lifted me off the ground and sent me on my way.

Blinking away the tears and gently rubbing my bottom to ease the pain, I knelt on the window seat staring out onto the High Street, wondering what I had done wrong. I also wondered what 'insolent' meant, but it was far too grown up a word for me to understand at that time.

Jeremy left Cleveland School soon after that and I grew up thinking it was because he kissed me. I decided that kissing was a bad thing to do. After all, I had never seen Mum and Dad do it.

The front lawn at Cleveland School.

My best friends at Cleveland School were Eleanor and Elizabeth. Both were daughters of doctors and Mum encouraged our friendship even though, as time went by, I realised Eleanor was a bully. Walking past the school gates on many a morning, I was met by a group of girls in my class huddled together on the path, waiting for me to get closer. Eleanor was always in the centre, organising their every move, and Elizabeth would be there too. My face dropped and my heart sank each time I saw 'the huddle' in the distance as I knew what was to come and it would affect me for the rest of the day.

'We're not talking to Anne Burton today,' was all Eleanor had to say and that was it. The group dispersed and everyone including Elizabeth looked down their noses at me and walked away without a word. I spent the rest of the day being ignored completely and feeling awful, wondering what I had done to deserve such nastiness.

Is it because I'm adopted? I thought, but I was sure Eleanor did not know.

Playtimes were agony as I wandered around alone, watching everyone else having fun and still wondering what was the matter with me. I didn't know how to make it better and instead waited for the next day when Eleanor would be all over me as if nothing had happened and all I could do was hope it would not happen again. It always did.

Eleanor, Elizabeth and I remained friends all through my time at Cleveland School because the good days far outweighed the bad. At weekends, when there were just the three of us in each other's houses, Eleanor was so friendly and such fun to be with. We would make up song and dance routines and put on shows for their parents but looking back I realise who always played the lead role; Elizabeth and I simply did as we were told. At nine years old, Eleanor passed an audition with flying colours for The Royal Ballet School in London, and I never saw her again. She left her mark on me though.

On days when it was an outside playtime, the teachers allowed us to wander around the grounds and sing and dance in certain parts of the woods, as long as we stuck to the rules regarding forbidden areas. We made dens together and collected moss and flowers for our pretend carpets, and the dens became our second homes that we returned to time and time again, acting out family life as we knew it.

The classes were small and studious with fifteen children in each, and by the time I was eight years old I was flying with the French language which I adored. Our French teacher was a tall, stringy, middle-aged lady with a grey bun called Mrs Onions, which we all found highly amusing. Partly because it was such a strange name to have but also because it fitted her job so well as a French teacher. Everywhere she went, she carried an enormous cloth bag with her which we firmly believed must be full of onions. Miss Cannon was our English teacher, a rotund woman with a red face, frizzy ginger hair and a body that suited her nickname. She was known as 'Cannonball' as she could erupt and boom at the slightest hint of any child expressing their individual personality in her lessons. Silence was insisted upon at all times, knuckles were occasionally rapped with a metal ruler she carried around the classroom and we were all scared stiff of her and her piercing blue eyes. Mrs Fitzsimmons, a silver-haired lady, was my form teacher and mathematics teacher too. All through my junior years she was frustrated and dismayed by my lack of understanding of basic maths, although I tried my best every day to understand. I really did. Maths was like another language to me and much harder than French, which of course *was* another language, though much more understandable.

I excelled in all other subjects and each school report praised me to the hilt. All Mum picked up on was the fact that my maths was not up to scratch and a tutor was found after she lectured me about not trying hard enough.

'Why you're no good at mathematics I'll never understand, Anne. I was top of the class at school.'

I wanted to shout and scream that our brains were not connected in any way, but kept quiet, having been taught to do so.

Why couldn't she hug me and say 'well done' for once, for all the other subjects I had excelled in each term? What was the point in hoping for that, though? I'd already worked out that any kind of praise from her would be a thing I hoped for in vain. My dad's reaction was a different kettle of fish. Poring over each report, with a big smile, he made up for Mum's attitude by hugging me and saying, 'Well done, Tish. That's my girl,' and it made me feel so proud.

He sat me down, took both my hands in his and explained that I did not have to be good at everything, saying, 'That's all anyone can ever do. Their best.'

Mum stood towering over us while he gushed praise on me and then she turned and walked away, tight-lipped as usual.

Once a week, I visited my Maths tutor – and guess where his huge house was? At last, a legitimate excuse to go to West Street without being reprimanded. My tutor, Colonel Morris, was a tall ex-army man with a ginger, handlebar moustache and greying ginger hair. He fitted the bill of a colonel exactly and his voice thundered across the room as he tried to teach me the basics of mathematics. It often rose to a crescendo as his frustration gathered momentum and he made me shudder with fear by the end of each lesson. He persevered, and I persevered, but my lessons came to an end a couple of years later, with me still flummoxed by anything mathematical. Another failure on my part. Another reason I was the imperfect daughter as far as Mum was concerned.

'All that money I spent on your lessons, and you still can't do it, you stupid girl,' was all she said, walking away once again.

In the summer at Cleveland School, our twice-weekly PE lessons consisted of country dancing outside on the front lawn. Most of the girls looked forward to it and the boys put up with it, looking awkward and embarrassed in their dancing shorts, with spindly white legs protruding from them and two left feet in the main.

Lunchtimes at Cleveland School were a set routine as at home, with the same meals being served on the same day each week. We all sat like little beavers in our dark brown and gold uniforms, nibbling away at meals dished up by the austere, white-coated dinner ladies. The school dining hall was overwhelming in its height and space, and with a prefect at the head of each table, bad manners, bad behaviour or any kind of raucousness was never contemplated. The only noise we could hear echoing around the hall was the clinking of cutlery, the quiet murmurings of friends yearning to socialise, and each child stacking their perfectly emptied plates onto huge stainless steel trolleys in the corner of the hall. That was until Fridays, when even the prefects allowed low moans and groans from the children they were supervising because we all knew what to expect for lunch. 'Floating fat' was the dish of the day. By the laws of probability, we all agreed that on one Friday in the future, a child *must* discover a piece of meat on their plate without fat attached.

How did the dinner ladies manage to achieve this dread of Fridays which encompassed the whole school?

Well, imagine white-coated witches stirring their cauldrons filled with watery, grey gravy, and a thick film of grease swirling around on the top. Inside the cauldron, you can spot pieces of fatty meat floating about with lumps of gristle firmly attached. Add to your image so far, the over-boiled potato mashed into large lumps and accompanied by soggy carrots, and then you may have the picture.

This unpalatable concoction was duly followed by rice pudding with a dollop of strawberry jam in the centre. It was the highlight of Friday lunchtimes for most children and everyone had their special way of eating it. Some of us drew patterns in the rice by pushing the jam in varying directions, others devoured the rice first saving the jam until after, and the sneaky ones who could get away with it mixed the jam and rice pudding to make the shade of pink that always came back to haunt us later in the day. I spooned mine in as fast as I could, trying not to take in the taste.

After a lunch like that, it was not surprising that someone always interrupted Friday afternoon assemblies by daring to vomit a thick splatter of pink sick, with carrots in it. Since those days at Cleveland School, I have noticed on my journey through life that there are always carrots in vomit. An abundance of them. Whatever you may have eaten, and it may not have included carrots, carrots always come back at you.

At the grand old age of seven, Mum let me travel to school and back on the service bus. Nearly every child that went from Yarm already did so and, finally, I was to become part of that independent community. It was so exciting to chat with friends on the top deck, but after a while I began to wish I had never asked. I sat with a friend called Maisie whose younger brother, George, always insisted on sitting near us. 'Nothing too wrong with that,' I hear you say, and I agree – to a point.

Maisie and George were the children of one of the local butchers and, as nice as they were, they perpetually smelt of meat and bones. Their parents smelt of meat and bones and their house smelt just the same. Their garden looked as if it was sprouting bones as they were strewn all over the lawn for the dogs to eat, and no doubt the occasional rat from the River Tees joined in.

I could put up with the way they smelt and still went to play at Maisie's house, but on our bus journeys home from school George outdid the rest of the family.

We all had seats which we claimed as our own for the two-mile journey to Yarm, and no one was allowed to move, once settled. Maisie and I sat upstairs on the second row from the back. George sat right behind us on the back row, alone. When I think back, I feel sorry for him. He must have needed a stomach referral since at least three times a week he got off the bus with his short trousers stained brown and dripping, and an unbelievable stench followed him. Poor George! I never heard what he ended up doing in later life. Perhaps one day, I will walk into a butcher's shop somewhere, recognise the man behind the counter from the smell he is exuding, and slink straight back out again, remembering those days on the bus.

I enjoyed my time at Cleveland School but much preferred helping in the shop, going out on deliveries with Dad, washing our car and all the practical tasks in life. When I was not helping, I was out playing with friends.

My friends were mostly children of other couples who ran businesses in Yarm and we all led a simple life. Going to their houses rather than inviting them to my house was a bonus, away from Mum's watchful eye. They all had brothers and sisters who played happily together, were silly and laughed together, sometimes they even argued with each other and showed all manner of emotions which Mum did not allow from me at home. I dreaded going back home and wished that I lived with my friends instead of

Mum. Their mums were all jolly ladies who let us be proper children, enjoyed being with us and even joined in with our games from time to time.

Sometimes Mum would insist that my friends came to our house to play and then hung around waiting to pounce. She would look for mistakes in my social interactions and point them out by belittling me, right there in front of them. Every time this happened, my face flushed and I stared at the floor, willing her to go away and hoping my friends did not see how embarrassed I was. It was impossible to be myself and have a good time with Mum in the same room.

I withdrew completely and took to playing in my bedroom rather than asking to go out, in case she insisted that my friends came to our house. Without them there, I spent hours alone. I played with the multitude of dolls that Santa had left over the years, even though dolls were not my thing, and they had never been on my Santa list. I created a whole new world for them, made out of net and scraps of material, lashed together with dowels and string. Two of the dolls became characters in a play, acting out all manner of scenarios with love and affection oozing from the 'mum doll' all day long. The 'child' won arguments against the 'mum' and was even able to get her to see the 'child's' point of view.

I was still lonely, even with my dolls around, and hated being an only child. I truly believed that somewhere in the world I had real brothers and sisters, and because I was so sure it made being alone even worse. Then my thoughts took over and interrupted the play. *Why was it only me that she gave away?*

Off I went into another world far away from my bedroom, staring into space with confusion filling my head and both dolls lying silent on the floor, watching me. Bringing myself back to reality, I invited three more dolls to join in; at last I had 'brothers and sisters' for a while and the room was full of chatter and mischief, with 'Mum' showing love to us all.

8

A Taste of Happiness

The family of dolls offered me love each time Mum withdrew her love and I sat alone in my bedroom, pretending to be happy. She must have been satisfied I was becoming the 'pink-kind-of-girl' she had hoped for, as I stopped asking Santa for train sets and a Scalextric because he always ignored my list.

In the real world, my life plodded along in a routine of school, Saturday visits to my Granny's farm and Sunday picnics with Mum and Dad. Occasionally, a friend of mine joined us. A friend that was chosen by Mum. I was still on edge and anxious when she was around, watching and waiting to find some reason to pounce. And pounce she did, many times. Some things we did together offered me freedom from her critical eye and the Sunday picnic was one of them.

Ridge Lane was our favourite destination – so named as the road was built on top of a ridge between two deep and scarily sheer wooded valleys on either side. Looking down out of the car window as Dad drove along, butterflies fluttered in my tummy wondering *what if...?*

It was an unbelievably narrow lane, with clumps of grass growing in the middle along its length and flanked by a few 'passing places' in the event of a vehicle coming the other way. The further we went along the lane, the steeper the switchbacks became, constructed in between the embankments that were carpeted with yellow primroses or bluebells depending on the time of year. The switchbacks were so steep and such fun and had us all wondering whether our car would make it up the other side. In the heart of the North Yorkshire moors, Ridge Lane cut through from the main Whitby road to Staithes, a small fishing village where our extended family owned a cottage.

Our choice of picnic spot remained the same on each visit: a wide, grassy verge positioned at the side of the lane underneath sycamore, oak and beech trees rustling in the ever-present breeze. A shallow stream meandered through the valley, way beneath our spot. The lane offered perfect peace apart from a few birds chattering in the trees and the occasional seagull from Staithes squawking as it flew past. Mum and Dad would relax on a 'checky blanket' reading their books, while my chosen friend and I would climb trees and make our way down the paths in the wooded valley to skim stones across the stream below, playing the afternoon away.

Our Sunday picnics always included mashed banana sandwiches which were a tempting, creamy yellow when first made, but invariably by the time we came to eat them, had festered into an uninviting black mush. Still, they were eagerly wolfed down with what verged on bad manners.

After eating, 'the walk' would be announced. Even Sunday picnics were not exempt. Dad tried his best to join in but often the effort was too great, and he turned a deathly shade of white. We would rest with him for a while until his colour returned as the little white heart tablet under his tongue did its job. Off we would go again, all of us knowing another rest would be needed soon. Other than seeing Dad suffering, Sundays in Ridge Lane were heaven.

After days like that, I would lie in bed humming pop songs to myself, reminiscing about the picnic, remembering the giggles, the fun and the rare sense of freedom that being out of earshot of Mum had given me. A feeling of peace would surround me as I drifted off to sleep, feeling happy that Dad had managed the walk and made it safely home for another week.

By the summer of my ninth year, Mum and Dad had invested in an old two-berth Sprite caravan which we towed to a site at Saltburn-by-the-Sea in

North Yorkshire, around twelve miles from Yarm. My nana joined us for that first outing, and all the way there she turned round to check the back window every few minutes, reassuring my dad by saying,

'It's still there Sandy,' to which he nodded and smiled.

This was a brand-new adventure for all of us, but I am sure my dad would have spotted the caravan detaching itself from the tow bar and rolling backwards along the road. Nana heaved a sigh of relief when we arrived, and we went to have a look around. My Dad, ever the peacemaker, tried to curb Mum's mutterings about the quality of the site, the kind of people staying there and the language that adults were using. I thought it looked fantastic as the sea was right on the doorstep and it was the open-air life I adored.

We stayed one night, and one night only, as it was too much for Mum to cope with when she opened the bedroom curtains the next morning. Right opposite, in another caravan, a man in a white string vest was frantically waving at her and mouthing 'Good Morning' alongside his wife sporting her pink rollers and a hair net. Mum gasped in disbelief and promptly turned away, shaking her head.

'I'm not staying here another night, Sandy, and putting up with people like that. They're so common.'

That was that. The decision was made, and we promptly packed up and went home.

It came as no surprise that Mum dismissed the idea of trying another site and Dad got the job of towing our caravan to Staithes, where we had spent many a holiday. The village was my second home, and I knew every nook and cranny of it and most of the villagers by name. Over the years, day trips to Staithes were aplenty and in the summer holidays, Mum, my cousin Dorothy and I stayed in the family cottage for a whole two weeks. Burton's Cottage, high up on one of the cliffs, had been left by my grandad in his will to Dad and his four sisters. The sisters hardly used it and it became our place to stay. Dad would join us on a Sunday when our shop was closed and occasionally stayed on, but usually it was just the three of us and Rex, our cocker spaniel.

This photo sums up the way I feel about the village of Staithes, even today. Spot the knock knees.

Mmm ... the salt tastes good.

Staithes village, nestled between two headlands, has two distinct sides to it with ancient cottages built into the cliffs. The main part of the village has a winding, cobbled high street with a smattering of cottages, shops and pubs. 'Overt Beck', which in posh vocabulary means 'over the other side of the beck', was accessed in those days by a dilapidated wooden footbridge which has since been replaced by a metal bridge. That side of Staithes mainly consists of a huge cliff called Cowbar, with a steep road wending its way up from the side of the beck to the top. Painted cottages, built into the front of the cliff, line the road upwards and at the very top there was an entrance to Dick Hick's allotment on top of the cliff itself. The Hicks were elderly friends of Mum and Dad who gave us permission to perch our newly acquired caravan at the edge of Dick's allotment, close to the entrance.

Why Dad wanted our caravan to be tethered down on top of a cliff was a mystery to me but many a happy weekend was spent there. The caravan took over from Burton's Cottage for a while as the place to stay, and in the school holidays Mum and I stayed on for the week while Dad went back to run our shop.

At first, I was anxious about being in such close proximity to Mum, day after day, in a caravan. I imagined the number of smacks that would land on my thighs when there was no one else there to supervise. I imagined after each smack and wondering once again what I had done to deserve such action. I also imagined being constantly tethered to her side and withdrawing into myself for fear of making a mistake and another slap landing. The first few days were 'prim and proper' days and then things changed. The village of Staithes was a safe place where I found whole days of freedom away from her. After sitting me down and pointing out the consequences of bad behaviour, she allowed me to go off with my friends who lived there, and we spent hours together.

'Cowbar', the cliff where our caravan was perched
is on the left of the photo.
'Staithes Sunrise' (photo by Stephen Hornsey).

If the tide was out, our first port of call was the rocks that surrounded the harbour. The mission began with us crouching down amongst them and, using wooden lollipop sticks saved from a previous treat, we prised off limpets and mussels to throw in our buckets. Once they were full, we raced over to 'sell' them from behind the counter of our 'fish and chip shop', which was perfectly formed from one of the weathered rocks. To restock our shelves, we sat on our haunches by favourite rock pools, catching starfish, winkles and whelks. Day after day, we collected shells from the beach on the way to our 'shop' and displayed them on the counter to entice more buyers. Once we had tired of 'selling', we would entertain ourselves by climbing up and down amongst the rocks, jumping off them, or simply sitting on them, popping seaweed to our hearts' content as we sat looking out over the harbour. If the tide was in, we would move further inland, running up and down the thousands of steep stone steps all over the village, just for fun. We explored path after path on one side of the Cowbar cliff, eventually hitting the steepest part where we walked sideways to stop us from sliding down through the bushes. Reaching the beck, we made paper yachts and set them off on the current to sail down towards the harbour, laughing and following them to see whose yacht would win without capsizing first.

Those days at Staithes were glorious. The one rule Mum put in place was to stay away from the sea, unless she was there with me, even though most of the fishermen and local families knew me. I stuck to that rule, as I knew once broken it would mean the end of my freedom and I understood where she was coming from.

Once a week when Dad arrived, those perfect days ended with us eating fish and chips, battered and fried in coal-fired fat burners from one of the shops in the village. The fisherwomen, wearing their Staithes bonnets, shook lashings of salt and vinegar onto them before wrapping them up in newspaper, and they smelt divine. The three of us would sit 'overt beck' and devour them in the open air – politely, of course, out of respect for Mum.

My new-found freedom came to an abrupt end when I was nine-and-a-half years old. A new family moved into a cottage overlooking the beach in Staithes and the two older girls, Megan and Celia, quickly befriended me. I doted on them from the outset and spent days tagging along and joining in with whatever they were doing. On one particular day, they decided to play a game of 'Dares', which involved taking turns to be dared to do something we would not normally do. I dared them to do pretty innocent things as I was new to this game. When it was my turn to be 'dared', both the girls huddled together whispering, then turned to me with straight faces, saying, 'Go and ask everyone on the beach if they are pregnant. If they say "no", call them a wanker.'

I looked up to those girls so much and did not even think to ask what either of the words meant. I knew they must have a reason for asking me to do it and being part of this game was exciting and made me feel wanted. I needed to appear brave by carrying out the dare so off I went to the beach with Megan and Celia watching me from the staith above. I scanned the beach to single out who to ask first and warily approached a couple sitting on a picnic rug, staring out to sea. Glancing up at the two big girls above me, I made my move.

'Excuse me,' I said in my bravest voice, and waited to get their attention. They turned to me smiling and were probably wondering what I was doing there. 'Are you pregnant?' I blurted out.

A look of confusion passed between them before the man shouted, 'Bugger off!' I was not sure what that meant either but could see from their faces it was not good, so I moved further along the beach asking the question again and again. If I got a negative response, I said what Megan and Celia had dared me to say before running off. By everyone's reactions, I was beginning to work out that they had tricked me into doing something really bad.

Mum appeared from nowhere and came flying down the steps onto the beach. An onslaught of smacks lifted each leg off the ground as I tried in vain to avoid them. With a grip like a vice, she hauled me off the beach without a word, marched me up the village high street and pulled me up a long flight of steps before she smacked me again and bundled me into Mrs Hick's house. There she laid into me good and proper and I knew I was in big, big trouble. Mrs Hick tried to defend me and told Mum to calm down as I pleaded with her to believe that I had no idea what the two naughty words meant. I was ashamed of myself for having been tricked into doing something so wrong, and Mum was ashamed that I could have done such a thing. She hardly spoke to me for the rest of our time at Staithes.

My loss of all freedom ensued and that hurt me – but nowhere near as much as the fact that the two girls had played me for a little fool. Another lesson learned early in life. Wait a while before placing your trust in anyone.

We hardly went to the caravan after that and I wondered if it was my fault, but nothing was ever said.

Dad towed the caravan to a farm nearer home. It was owned by Mr and Mrs Frank who were customers of ours and had become friends. The Franks' farm was one of the many far-flung farms that we delivered to and I had often been there with Dad or 'Vic the Spiv'. During the school holidays, Mrs Frank sometimes invited me to stay and play with their three children.

About four miles from our shop, the farm lay at the end of a country lane through open countryside. Driving towards their farm was like going into another world. A world lined with enormous farms and surrounded by fields growing various crops, cows and sheep peacefully grazing, and in spring, of course, little lambs leaping high up into the air, bleating excitedly. Along the entire length of the lane, there were hawthorn hedgerows protecting birds' nests and it was ablaze with wild flowers. Rabbits and other wildlife scurried about and, at the right time of year, we had to avoid pheasants holding a death wish as they plodded across the road, right in front of our car.

The entrance to the farm had sturdy wooden gateposts at either side of a cattle grid, and the clanking of the metal bars against the tyres signified that we were nearly there. With only another half mile to go through the fields and past the farm workers' cottages, the Franks farmhouse came into view.

As we approached the farmhouse and outbuildings, we skirted past a magnificent old copper beech tree near their orchard. I loved its symmetrical shape, its amazing colours and the peace it offered me as I spent more time at the Frank's farm. I thought of it as my tree, a tree to climb as high as I dare, and most wonderful of all, a tree with a perfectly horizontal branch near its base, thick and strong enough for me to hang upside down on and drift away into my adopted thoughts for what seemed like hours. My thoughts would be interrupted by one of the Frank children calling me to go and play.

Years of treasured happiness followed at the farm, enjoying the company of Jennifer, their daughter, and their two sons, Richard and Christopher. I loved being with them and it made such a change from being the only one in adult company, or the only one, full stop. Hanging upside down on my tree, I also thought about the Frank family and marvelled at how they belonged to each other. They looked like each other, they talked like each other and they laughed at the same things. They were a proper family.

Jennifer taught me to ride Duke, her beautiful chestnut pony. We started off walking and trotting around the muddy farmyard and progressed to the fields and cantering. I helped her to feed and groom him and the smell and warmth as I nuzzled into his neck made me smile. The four of us played cricket together in a field at the front of the farm. This field went right down to the River Tees and seemed to go on forever. Mr Frank mowed our 'cricket pitch' to within an inch of its life and it was even more fun to play the game than sitting watching the test matches with my dad before the *Six O'Clock News* at home. On those delightful days at the farm, I learned to bowl overarm and send the ball spinning at speed towards whoever was batting. I learned to field and enjoyed running like the wind to catch the ball, cupping it in my hands and diving towards the grass, screaming 'out!' at the top of my voice, roaring with laughter. My emotions ran wild and it felt good. I felt like *me*.

Batting was the best and I had a keen eye for the ball. I hit many a six even though there was no boundary – only the River Tees – and I loved launching myself towards the wicket to stay in play. Other children from nearby farms would come and join in our game and it was heaven. I felt so free. We all laughed together, played together, and it didn't seem to matter how scruffy and dirty we were. Best of all there was not a frilly, frothy dress or a skirt in sight.

Over time I was invited to stay the night, even though some weekends Mum and Dad would be in our caravan just around the corner in the orchard. Mrs Frank welcomed me into her fold with a beaming smile, telling Mum, 'One more won't make any difference.'

She was used to feeding the 'five thousand' including her own family, the farm workers and anyone else that dropped in. The farm kitchen was enormous with a long wooden table in the middle of it, capable of seating at least twelve people. An old cast-iron cooking range spanned one wall, with a thick tin kettle simmering on a hot plate at the edge of the coal fire. Walking into their kitchen was like walking into happiness. The homely smell of Mrs Frank's baking wafted up into my nostrils and hung around the kitchen all day long. For breakfast we poured lashings of warm milk onto our cornflakes, collected from the cows in the dairy minutes before, and it was unbelievably creamy and comforting. Mrs Frank produced pies, scones and cakes from nowhere and they kept on coming. Perhaps that is why she was a perfect picture of a farmer's wife in my eyes. She was plump and jolly and ran her farm kitchen in a laid-back and unhurried way. She was never flustered, she never shouted and always had a huge smile for her children and for me too. She seemed like a proper mum to me.

Mr Frank looked exactly the opposite to her. He was tall and skinny with the biggest hands I have ever seen. They were reddened and battered from all the manual work on the farm and he constantly wore a flat cap and wellies. On entering the farmhouse, his wellies were deposited next to the others, standing in a long line in the porch, by the big back door. Mr Frank was a smiley person too and loved having his children around. We all had jobs to do and got involved in helping – especially at harvest time.

We used to spend our days off school out in the fields with Mr Frank and his farmhands. One of them would cut the corn using the red Massey Ferguson combine harvester. Going anywhere near that massive machine was forbidden, so instead we had a whale of a time sitting in the trailer, hooked onto the back of the tractor which another farmhand drove alongside the combine harvester. This enormous contraption had a long red chute aimed towards the trailer we were sat in. The first thrill of the day was bouncing along the field with our ears pricked, listening for the corn coming up the chute towards us. As it rose, our eyes widened with anticipation, and the noise of the corn volcano erupted. All this happened within seconds. The sight of it pouring out of the top of the chute and into the trailer next to us caused screeches and laughter. Our eyes were glued to it as it became a solid stream, separating into kernels as it hit the bottom. Our hands flew to our noses to shield them as the cloud of corn dust enveloped us, and we all started to sneeze uncontrollably. Then more excitement as the mountain of corn grew deeper by the second, and we flung ourselves around the trailer to avoid being buried. All the while we laughed and laughed, and once again I couldn't believe how happy I felt. Happy and free. Sometimes we were very daring and would go too near the red chute and allow ourselves to be hit by the stream of corn that battered our young skin.

Just before break time, Jennifer and I raced back across the fields to the farm kitchen. Mrs Frank handed us two wicker baskets filled with homemade crusty bread, scones and other goodies along with some metal urns of milky tea. Sitting down in the fields, the tea washed the dust out of our throats, and we took our fair share of food I have to say. None of us children particularly liked the taste of the tea, but it did not matter one bit. We were all together having fun. After each trailer was full of corn, we rode back to the farm perched on top of it, happy as sandboys and, climbing down, we watched as the farmhand tipped the trailer to pour the corn into the granary. At the end of each day, and always after he pretended he had to be persuaded, Mr Frank let us slide down the corn mountain in the granary, once and once only. We never abused that 'once only' decision or asked for more. Those days of freedom and laughter are etched into my memory. The bonus was that no one was watching and waiting to pounce if I made a mistake. No one was listening to correct me or scold me for using the wrong word. I had no bows in my hair, no lacy socks and I was allowed to wear trousers and wellies all day long.

It did not matter to us that we all came home scratched and itchy with our knees prickling from the corn husks, and that we still had the job of collecting the eggs from the hen huts in the barn, after tea. The Frank children felt like my family and those were the days when the skies were always blue.

Every Bonfire Night, both our families gathered in the apple orchard at the side of the farmhouse. Mrs Frank and Mum donned their pinnies and leant out of our caravan window to serve us hot dogs and onions in a bun, and mountains of baked beans along with foil-covered jacket potatoes, cooked at the edge of the bonfire. We all stood round and marvelled at the guy we had made that year wearing Mr Frank's old clothes. It sat precariously on top of the bonfire looking at us from underneath its straw hairdo and flat cap.

'It looks a bit like you, Dad,' the Frank children yelled each year, grinning, and no one was upset by their comment. It *did* look like him, as Mr Frank's hair was bright ginger too.

Both dads took turns to light the fireworks and we would 'woooo' and 'weeee' at each shower of colour shooting up into the sky and, together with the smell of the gunpowder hanging in the air, Bonfire Nights at their farm were unforgettable. One year my dad was forced to play the superhero when a spent rocket landed on the sleeve of my brand-new red furry anorak and instantly set it alight. He ripped it off me within seconds, threw it onto the grass and stomped on it until it stopped burning. Dad saved me that night and all that remained of my furry anorak was a molten mess on the ground.

Being with the Frank children made me wonder more about my roots and identity. I often lay in bed questioning whether I really did have brothers and sisters of my own somewhere, and if I did, would they look like me, talk like me and think like me? I imagined chatting to them without feeling anxious about being scorned or belittled. I know that real families may not work like that but I imagined, if I found them one day, perfect happiness could be mine and I would never be lonely again.

('Crest of a Wave' – Ralph Reader – 1934)

9

Christmas

At nine years old and a full year before my time, Cleveland School entered me for the eleven-plus exam. If I passed it, Yarm Grammar School would be the next chapter in my life. This school was not far up The Spital, the bank where my dad still struggled on our obligatory Sunday walks.

At parents' evening the term before, Mrs Fitzsimmons explained that my mathematical talent had finally surfaced and I stood a good chance of passing the exam. *Hallelujah,* I could almost hear Mum thinking. Finally, this imperfect daughter of mine has done something right.

The importance of the exam was drummed home throughout the Christmas holidays. Mum made me revise for five hours each day apart from Christmas Day and Boxing Day. I resented the fact I had to revise, but at that age I took Mum's commands lying down. For the first few days of the holidays, my friends came to call for me but were turned away.

On Christmas Eve, Mr and Mrs Best invited us to go through the dividing door on the first-floor landing to the 'other side' of the house, where they were having a get-together. All dressed accordingly, Dad unlocked the door to the 'other side' and we joined them in their lounge above The Café. A few other familiar faces were already there and, as usual, Mum beckoned me to sit at her feet which on this occasion was next to the Best's electric fire. Chatter about Christmas followed, with everyone sharing their plans for the festive period. Mr Best offered the grown-ups a drink and my dad declined, explaining that as a Methodist, he was teetotal. Mr Best laughed and cajoled him to 'join in with the festive spirit'.

Dad reluctantly agreed to have a small glass of sherry. Mum had her Christmas gin and tonic and the chatter carried on.

Simon Best was sat opposite me on the floor. Slightly older than me, he had white-blonde hair, icy blue eyes and skin like a ghost, apart from two pink circles on his cheeks. He kept glancing at me with a smirk on his face. I did not understand why, so I avoided his gaze completely.

My thoughts drifted away from the Christmas chatter to a day when I had played cricket with him and three of his friends in our shared backyard. The size of a tennis court, it was enclosed on two sides by our three-storey house and on the other two sides by a ten-foot wall, separating us from 'The Skinyard' at the rear. That day, Simon was batting, and I was told to bowl. The other three boys strategically placed themselves around our yard in fielding positions. Little did Simon know I was an experienced cricketer, courtesy of The Frank family, and when he missed the first ball, his icy blue eyes glared at me as his brow furrowed with concentration. Ball after ball went past him. I could see the pink circles on his cheeks flushing and spreading as his anger started to build. As I propelled the ball towards him again, with increasing accuracy and confidence, his face contorted and he managed to hit it with a flailing swing that was much too hard for the space in our yard. If he had aimed for a window it would have been smashed to smithereens but his aim was much closer to home. He was aiming for my face. The cricket ball smashed straight into my left eye. I burst into tears, and he ran over wagging his finger at me, laughed right in my face and shouted, 'Think you're better than me, Anne Burton? You'll never be better than me. You're just a girl ... and anyway ... you're adopted!'

As I ran inside, sobbing with pain, I swore to myself I would never play with him again. He had hurt me so badly and that was nothing to do with my eye. *How does he even know I'm adopted?* I thought, *Mum can't have told them, can she?*

Returning from my daydream to the conversation in the lounge, I heard Mrs Best say my name, 'Anne, would you like a drink?'

I replied, quite innocently asking for one of the two drinks I associated with Christmas. 'Please may I have a Bristol Cream?' I said, and everyone in the room burst out laughing.

Mum looked horrified. Dad looked bemused, but I could see from his expression he was finding it hard to keep a straight face. It was the consensus of everyone in the room, fuelled by a little alcohol, that as it was Christmas, I should be allowed to try a small glassful. Mum and Dad didn't have a leg to stand on. And so it came to pass, that at nine years old, by the warmth of the Best's three-bar electric fire, I tried my first alcoholic beverage. Mrs Best handed me a pretty crystal glass, half full of this brown liquid, and smiled at me saying, 'We don't have any Bristol Cream so will Croft be alright?'

I nodded shyly and thanked her as more laughter filled the lounge. My nostrils were hit by the overpowering smell of liquorice, and I wished I had asked for a glass of lemonade. I looked around for clues as to what to do next. Mum was glaring at me, willing me to put the glass down on the hearth and apologise, but I could not back down now. I took a big breath, lifted the glass to my lips and downed it in one just like shot drinkers do nowadays. Immediately, I felt a warm flush going right through my body and my cheeks began to burn. I felt woozy and distant from all the chatter but it felt quite nice. I could not stop myself from giggling with gusto at the grown-up jokes filling the room. I looked up at Mum and ignored her glares and continued listening to jokes I did not understand, but I was happy and joining in for the first time in my life instead of being 'the listener'. The sherry had given me confidence.

Within minutes, Mum made her apologies and pushed me back through the dividing door on the landing. She pronounced me drunk and put me to bed. I cannot remember how I felt on Christmas Day morning, but I enjoyed that alcoholic wooziness and the confidence it offered me. Mum gave me breakfast as usual and nothing was mentioned – but her face said it all.

Christmas Day: that special day of the year when Jesus was born and all good parents have put up a tree. A tree which their children have decorated and danced around, screeching with delight and imagining the Christmas to come. Well, that is how it was in the films I had seen on the television.

Unfortunately, Christmas was not like that in our house. I was lucky enough to have a real Christmas tree, but each year Mum carried the two wooden boxes of decorations into the dining room, half-closed the door and decorated our tree all by herself. Once finished, she opened the door with a Christmas smile and exclaimed to the child waiting in the wings, 'Look at the tree! Isn't it pretty?'

It always looked beautiful and I wondered why she never asked me to help her decorate it and let me be her little girl for a while. It would have been so exciting. One Christmas, catching her in a good mood and planning ahead for the following year, I dared to broach the subject. Her mood changed immediately. She looked at me, raising her eyebrows, and said, 'No, Anne, you'd put things in the wrong place. It's better to let me do it … and much quicker.'

What's the wrong place? I wondered, *what do you mean?* It was only a Christmas tree after all, so why did the decorations have to be in a certain place?

I could have used my imagination and put my homemade fairy back on top of the tree where she belonged. Each year I waited to see if Mum took her out of the wooden box. When I first made the fairy at school, it took pride of place at the top of the tree, watching over us all through Christmas, and I felt so proud. Every year after that, I could see her lying alone on top of the decorations in the box as Mum carried them through to the dining room, but she never quite made it out, and I was disappointed that my fairy was not good enough for Mum either.

Christmas Day is also a time for surprise presents and families to be happy together, or so I believed. That did not happen in our house either. In November each year, Mum passed me some notepaper and told me to make my 'Santa list', which I loved doing and I decorated it with such care for him. Each year he came and left our house without bringing anything from my list, and I began to wonder why.

Is it because I haven't been good enough? I would ask myself, but I would never know and how could I ask Santa when no one ever saw him?

Each year, he left a shiny red apple, an orange, some monkey nuts and two presents in a pillowcase at the end of my bed, so I knew he had been when I woke up on Christmas Day. Even when I was sixteen, Santa still arrived with his nuts! Mum and Santa must have discussed those two presents in detail on Christmas Eve, as she always knew so much about them; so much, in fact, that she was itching to let the secret out.

On Christmas Day, year after year, Mum told Dad and me to sit in a circle (an extremely small circle) on the lounge carpet. We then waited for the next instruction.

'Right then. We'll take turns to open our presents in order. Dad first because he's the oldest,' and then the ceremony began, after she added, 'Make sure you do it carefully so I can iron the paper for next year … and put the tags in a pile for your thank-you letters, Anne.'

After Dad and I opened each of our presents, there was an uneasy silence until Mum heard the words, 'Thank you. It's just what I wanted.'

I longed to rip the paper off my presents and fling it all over the room. What was so wrong with a floor full of ripped wrapping paper, and happy faces with eyes shining? That would have been Christmas to me.

In our house excitement and silliness were forbidden. Surprises were forbidden too, it seemed. Opening both of my presents each year, I tried so hard to block out Mum's voice telling me what was inside them before I had even unravelled one corner of the paper. It totally spoilt the surprise and nothing could stop her. With each passing Christmas, my frustration grew, and I understood less and less why Santa needed my list at all.

I was different from Mum and kept her presents as a surprise. I spent hours perfecting them. At six years old, I made her a dressing-table mat with the word 'Mum' stitched right across the centre, in red and yellow cross-stitch. At seven, I pricked my finger a hundred times sewing a patchwork pincushion together. When I was eight, I knitted her a scarf which seemed to take for ever and all my pocket money to buy the wool. She smiled when she got my presents, so I suppose that was a bonus, but the eyes that said 'thank you' never looked into mine. Instead, they looked right past me, still searching for that perfect daughter.

My dad was thrilled with whatever I bought him, and his hugs nearly crushed me. Pipe cleaners one year, a box of feathered flies for his fishing trips the next year – but his favourite present was undoubtedly the red and yellow maggots, the year after that. Fresh and plump-looking, those maggots wriggled about in their brown paper bag, eyeing me up as I sat on the top deck of the bus coming back from Stockton, and they went down a storm. I sneaked them into the back of one of the fridges in the shop and wrapped them up just in time for our opening ceremony. I got blasted by Mum for that. I tried to explain that I knew my dad would be thrilled with them but that was 'beside the point' and wrong, again.

'Come on, it's Christmas, Madge. Don't be so hard on her all the time,' pleaded Dad, but I had set the mood for the day.

I got to play with any games that Santa brought me for an hour or so and then it was time to tidy up, put on a flouncy dress and have ribbons put in my hair, ready to visit my dad's stepmother for Christmas lunch.

Auntie Hilda, as I called her, was a robust woman at least six foot tall, with a short, greying bob, horn-rimmed glasses, and looked more like a man to me. She was very staunch, but at least she had a sense of humour and loved children. In her hallway stood a highly-polished copper gong suspended on a low stand which I was allowed to 'dong' six times with all my might when Christmas lunch was ready each year. On arrival, the grown-ups would migrate to the parlour and, after giving all my relations a kiss and a hug, I ended up at Mum's feet, as usual. They sat around, each sipping their single glass of *Bristol Cream* sherry and chatting about people I did not know and things I did not understand. My male cousins went off into the dining room to watch carols being sung on the television. How I wished I could join them instead of pretending to listen to the grown-ups' unintelligible conversations before their attention turned to me.

'How is school?' one of my aunties would ask.

Another would take over, 'Have you read any good books lately, Anne?'

I never knew how to answer because whatever my reply, it was rarely the right one for Mum, and I stood sharply corrected in front of them all. My answers faded away by the end of the sentence because I could feel her eyes on me as the confidence to get it all out was waning. As I got older, the look on my relations' faces told me they were uncomfortable with the way Mum constantly corrected me but nothing was ever said. One year, I asked if I could go and help Auntie Hilda in the kitchen and all eyes turned to Mum, wondering if my request would be sanctioned. It was either that one glass of *Bristol Cream* that mellowed her or the knowledge that my relations were waiting to see what her response would be, but whatever it was, permission was granted. From then on, the Christmas visit to Auntie Hilda's took a turn for the better.

She showed me how to put together simple things like sausages with bacon wrapped around them – now known as pigs in blankets – and how to mix a delicious, fruit-laden stuffing and spread it into a baking tray ready for the oven. She was a trained *Cordon Bleu* cook and, from her tiny kitchen, she produced a mouth-watering Christmas lunch for eleven of us without any soggy vegetables in sight.

There was a roaring log fire on Christmas Day in the dining room and even though the house had no central heating, the doors to the shabby Victorian conservatory were opened halfway through the meal to cool the room down. The whole house was crumbling around Auntie Hilda's ears, but she made sure that Christmas Day lunch with all its trimmings was delicious.

Her Christmas tablecloth was cheery and festive with a mountain of crackers at one end, and all of the children were trusted with a delicate, pale green water glass. A brass clock, two-foot high and encased in a cracked and sellotaped glass dome, stood on the long wooden sideboard. It was a replica of Cologne cathedral and it entirely fascinated me. Its chimes softly struck the hour and half hour as we ate, and watching its moving parts count the hours remains a vivid memory of being at Auntie Hilda's house.

Christmas lunch was a happy occasion as all my dad's sisters had a wicked sense of humour, just like him, and Mum was outnumbered when trying to calm down everyone's raucous laughter.

After ploughing through their four-course meal, all the grown-ups offered to do the washing up and every year they were told to wait until Auntie Hilda and I had organised the dirty dishes in the kitchen. Then she announced with a big smile,

'I think the men can wash up this year!' which they were expecting to hear anyway.

Auntie Hilda percolated the coffee and unveiled the cheese selection, ready for our fifth course of cheese and biscuits.

One year Mum remarked loudly, 'Anne never helps in the kitchen at home,' which was totally untrue. Auntie Hilda smiled and, after Mum left the room, whispered in my ear with a chuckle, 'I wonder why?'

Those three words gave me the courage to confide in Auntie Hilda, as I told her, 'I've asked Mum to teach me how to cook, but she says it's quicker to do it herself. I really enjoy helping you Auntie Hilda because you don't shout at me all the time.'

Auntie Hilda bent down and gently hugged me.

After Christmas lunch she would invite us back into the parlour and, surrounded by her cluttered collection of Victorian ornaments, we would sing carols while she hammered away on the battered old piano.

Then the whole family opened their presents and Mum was unable to spoil the surprises as she had no idea what was being given to me.

Dusk fell, and each year that meant it was time to move twelve miles along the road to Auntie Doris's for Christmas tea.

My Auntie Doris and Uncle Ted owned Elmridge Gardens, a market garden on the north side of Darlington. They had built it up from a single potting shed and, over the years, extended as they could afford to do it. When they retired, they had one of the biggest market gardens and flower shops in the North East of England.

They invited me to stay for a few days at a time in the school holidays, and I adored helping the staff, learning how to do flower arrangements, bouquets and wreaths.

Auntie Doris was extremely bossy and had a gammy leg – whatever that meant – which we children had to be careful not to knock. She was my dad's youngest sister and from her sense of humour and her kindness towards me, I could see Dad in her, through and through.

During those Christmas visits, my dad looked tired and pale and sat listening to all the chatter around him, probably waiting to go home. I am sure he would have loved to rest on Christmas Day, one of his few days off in the year, but it was tradition for us to go visiting and that kept the family together. Also, Mum loved to boast on those occasions about how well the shop was doing – but that was not the case at all.

Getting back home on Christmas night, I arranged all my presents in a neat pile under the tree, ready for Boxing Day.

The Boxing Day cocktail party was a glamorous affair and because it was a buffet, I was allowed to help prepare it. It was a night-time affair for all my fake 'aunties and uncles' that had got to know us as customers and evolved into friends. Two by two they drifted in and I stood in awe surrounded by their elegance. The men in their dark suits, sporting velvet dickie bow ties and looking like they had walked straight off a James Bond film set. On their arm were their red-lipped wives with swept up hair and the highest of heels, wearing beaded cocktail dresses of a fashionable length allowing a glimpse of their nylon-clad knees. A distinct smell of hairspray wafted in after them, mingled with the scent of Chanel No. 5 and Tweed. Swirling smoke from long cigarette holders soon joined forces with thicker smoke from cigars and made its way upwards to form a blue haze, high on our dining room ceiling. Glasses clinked as the celebration of the party began, with only my dad abstaining from alcohol.

There was Uncle Jack, an engineer with his ginger handlebar moustache who spat when he spoke and drank whisky until he could barely walk and had to be helped home by his wife, Auntie Kath. Unlike her husband, she drank gin, and they staggered off down the High Street together after each party.

Uncle John, a plump, wholesale greengrocer, drank beer before graduating onto whisky and insisting on lifting me up and throwing me higher and higher towards the ceiling with the more he drank, until fear overcame the excitement. His tiny blonde wife, Auntie Doreen, was a bit of a flirt – and so was Uncle John – but as there was no one interesting to flirt with apart from Mum and Dad, that's what happened. Dad hated it when Auntie Doreen's attention turned to him, but I could see Mum was flattered by Uncle John's interest as her eyes twinkled and she smiled a real smile for once.

Uncle George, spoke posh and was a director of Jackson's bakery, whose sliced bread we stocked in our shop. He drank anything in sight while puffing on a Jimmy Savile size cigar, gambled like mad, and was always in a rush to get somewhere else. When he got there, he was always in a rush to get away. Auntie Denise, his long-suffering wife who was the double of Ingrid Bergman, always offered me a squirt of her Chanel while explaining about pulse points. I adored talking to her and the feeling was mutual.

Uncle William (Mr Frank from the farm) seldom drank and talked to my dad for most of the evening, and Auntie Betty (Mrs Frank) always brought her wonderful baking to add to the already groaning buffet table.

As the party got into full swing, I sat in my corner, watching and listening until I heard Mum shout above the chatter, 'Come on, Anne, time to make yourself useful. Offer these canapés around and be polite. Don't forget to smile … and keep the plate level, for goodness sake!'

Auntie Denise stood up for me and shouted back, 'She's the best waitress in Yarm, Margaret. You know that. And she's always polite.'

Those parties were strange affairs. There was no music and no dancing. Instead, there was a seriousness in the chatter from the wives about such things as the virtue of the non-stick pan, the marvel of the twin-tub washing machine and the ease of entertaining after splashing out on an electric coffee percolator. I chose to sidle over to hear the men's watered-down jokes, discussions about sport and Dad's latest story of the goings-on in the shop which had the men doubling over with laughter. I followed suit.

'Tell us the tarantula tale again, Sandy,' laughed Uncle George and they all started to wince as he exaggerated and told them, wide-eyed, of the size of the tarantula Uncle John had unknowingly delivered to our shop, hidden in the depths of a wooden banana crate from his greengrocer's warehouse in Stockton. The tarantula's proportions grew each year as Dad took the stage.

After a while Mum would declare the buffet open and as plates clattered and glasses were refilled, my job was to set the chairs straight around the edge of the room so everyone could sit and eat and compliment Mum on her food. As the hours went by, the drinking increased until the majority ended up sozzled and loud. Then they went home. I was fascinated and confused by parties like these, watching Mum letting go, laughing and enjoying herself. The façade soon slipped as the last party-goers left, the smile disappeared and her back straightened as she regained control of her own personality.

'Well, it all seemed to go well, Sandy. I think everyone was impressed, don't you? So nice to have well-to-do friends. Time to start the clearing up now and time for you to disappear, Anne. It's way past your bedtime.'

Over the years, three things stood out to me when reflecting on those parties. The first was that Mum was like two different people. There was the side that she offered to the outside world, which was charitable and happy, and the darker side which was what Dad and I lived with, within our four walls. The party also taught me that men's down-to-earth conversations about sport and daft goings-on fascinated me more than talk about material things, verging on snobbery. The main thing I knew was that I was not posh. My roots were not posh.

'How did you know that?' I hear you ask.

Somewhere deep down inside me, I just knew.

On Boxing Day, before I was allowed any thoughts of helping with the food or joining in with the forthcoming party, I had a task to fulfil. Straight after breakfast, Mum instructed me to gather up my presents along with the pile of tags from under the tree and settle down to write my thank-you letters in the dining room. It took me hours to write those letters as I did not know what to say. Everything I thought of saying had been said the day before, when I had received the presents and thanked everybody. Mum would pop her head around the door from time to time and, with a frown, ask why I was taking so long.

'Please come and help me,' I wanted to say but I kept my head down. Sometimes my thoughts took over as I wondered, *why can't I write them when I've had a chance to play with my presents and then I'll have more to say?*

Mum seemed to delight in taking away any enjoyment of getting my presents in the first place and not allowing me time to look at them. Then I would feel guilty for having such thoughts and battled on. I must admit it felt good putting my fountain pen down after writing that last thank-you letter. It felt even better knowing there was a month's grace before the next round of letters to be written, after my birthday. Perhaps starting and finishing a task was what Mum was trying to drum into in me, and it worked. To this day, I feel guilty if I don't finish what I have started, whether it is the ironing, the cleaning, the decorating or even a bottle of wine!

In the first week of January 1964, I took the eleven-plus exam. It was in two halves on two separate days. I passed the first half but failed the second, so back to the drawing board.

As soon as Mum opened the letter telling her the results, she called me into the kitchen, prodded my chest with one finger and pushed me onto a chair saying, 'Just as I thought. I knew you would fail.'

('The Fairy on the Christmas Tree' – Gracie Fields – 1939)

('Lonely Pup in a Christmas Shop' – Adam Faith – 1960)

('River' – Joni Mitchell – 1971)

10

Being Part of the Gang

The following January, at the age of ten, I retook the eleven-plus exam and surprisingly – as I could not do anything right in Mum's eyes – I passed with flying colours. She managed to congratulate me, then added,

'Now for the hard work at the Grammar School, Anne, or it'll all have been a waste of time.' *What will?* I thought, but soon understood she meant the money already spent for my private education at Cleveland School.

A week or so after, Dad presented me with a magnificent replacement to the squeaky, old blue bike I had been riding from the age of six years old. Over the years, he had adjusted the handlebars and the seat up to their highest possible position, but my legs continued to sprout at an alarming rate and my knees were nearly up round my chin as I rode it.

'Well done pet, you deserve it,' he said as he ushered me into our backyard with a grin on his face, to show me my new bike.

And what a bike it was! I instantly fell in love with it and promised my dad that I would cherish it. In front of me stood a gleaming blue-and-white Royal Enfield bicycle, proudly balancing on its very own stand. It looked huge, but as I sat on it for the first time, we could both see that my bike and I were a perfect fit. Dad showed me round it, pointing out the pump nestled in its holder and the light on the front handlebar. He asked me to test both sets of brakes and then off I went around the yard.

'Don't squeeze the front brakes too hard,' he said laughing, 'remember what happened on your tricycle when you were four. That gash on your forehead took ages to mend.'

Round and round the yard I rode, and round and round again, feeling like a proper princess and listening to Dad chattering happily.

'Royal Enfield make motorbikes as well, you know. The best motorbikes in the whole world so you'll be able to fly like the wind. Your Mum and I had one when we were courting, have I ever told you that?' he called out, and I could see that he was as excited as me with his purchase.

Mum came down from the kitchen to join us, but only to remind me of my unfinished homework and tell me to put my bike away for the night. Dad and I glanced at each other with our shared understanding that it was best to obey.

My bike and I travelled miles that summer. Along with friends, I explored the sweet-smelling lanes around Yarm, flying down the steep hills and pedalling like crazy to reach the top at the other side, stopping for a break to sit and chat by streams and generally having a wonderful time. For the first time in years, I felt free. I adored my new bike. Each Sunday after chapel, I set to work in the yard, washing and polishing my newly acquired friend. I sluiced the dried mud off the tyres to let the whitewall effect shine through. I pumped them up to the correct poundage, courtesy of Dad's basic maintenance lessons which included a practical on 'How to Mend a Puncture in the Middle of Nowhere'. I rubbed all the chrome work with cleaner, including each of the many spokes on both wheels, and polished it off, after which I stood back and admired my beautiful bike, all ready to go for my next ride out into the country.

It was not long before it was taken off me. My freedom vanished in an instant and I was confined to my room for three weeks. Speeding flat out down The Spital, heading for home, my friend Geraldine suggested we call in to see her dad on his allotment. This was right next to Yarm Grammar School where I was due to begin the new chapter in my life five weeks later. His patch was to the rear of the allotments, and we left our bikes propped up against the gated brick wall and went in. Right in front of us, a tall, green bush heaving with 'plumptious' pea pods beckoned us to taste its delights. We looked at each other with questioning eyes. They were there for the taking and there was no one in sight. We glanced around, knowing what our next move had to be.

'They won't miss a few, will they?' I said.

'Come on then, we'll have to be quick before Dad spots us,' whispered Geraldine, and we launched ourselves onto the ground in front of the bush. Ready to attack, we reached for some pods.

Pulling three off, we instantly froze as a gruff voice behind us bellowed, 'What do you think you're doing? Get up and come here … and give me those peas. That's called pinching, do you know that?'

A balding, middle-aged man as tall as a giant, and dressed in a blue, boiler suit, grabbed both of us by the scruffs of our necks, almost lifting us off the ground, and without a word, hauled us back through the gate that led to the allotments.

Spotting our bikes, he calmly walked over to them announcing, 'Well, these are both confiscated. You can have them back after we've been to the police station.' We stood stock-still, shaking in our shoes.

'Alright, you can go first,' he said, nodding at me, 'what's your name and where do you live?'

I was petrified but managed to blurt out my name and that of our shop. The man took a long, hard look at me, folded his arms and said, 'So you're Mr Burton's daughter are you? What do you think he'll make of you pinching peas? I can tell you now, he won't be pleased.' I hung my head, speechless.

'And who are you?' he said, switching his gaze to Geraldine. When she told him, things got worse, as he said, 'Do you want me to go and get your dad and then you can tell him what you've both been up to?'

Eyes wide, we looked up at him shaking our heads and then suddenly I found my voice. 'Mum'll kill me if she finds out. Please, Mister, give us a chance. We'll never do anything like this again.' Geraldine's head was nodding so hard in agreement, I expected it to fall off and land by his feet.

'If I ever see you in these allotments again … and never mind visiting your dad anymore,' he said looking at Geraldine, 'I'll have you both for pinching and next time I *will* take you to the police station. Do you hear me?'

We both muttered, 'Yes, Mister,' with our heads firmly directed towards the footpath.

Waving us away he said, 'Off you go then and make sure you go straight home.'

The Pea Pinching Episode was behind us, or so we believed, and we leapt onto our bikes and shot off into Yarm High Street, still shaking.

The following day, Dad called me down to the shop. In front of the counter stood our local bobby, who proceeded to reprimand me and warn me against pursuing a life of crime before he turned on his heel and, with a peremptory nod to Dad, went on his way. I stood there shaking and wondering what would happen next.

'Your Mum needs to know,' was all Dad said, as she appeared from the back of the shop and another slap landed.

This time it was right across my left cheek and the disappointment in her eyes bored into mine, as she screamed, 'How dare you bring our name down, Anne? It'll be all around Yarm within no time. That's it! Your bike's going away and you can stay in for three weeks. Now, get out of my sight.'

On that day, three pea pods cemented the fact that pinching is wrong, and for each pea pod, I forfeited a week of my summer holidays.

September arrived, and a new chapter of my life awaited me as I walked up The Spital on that first morning towards Yarm Grammar School. The gate to the allotments was ajar and I hurried past, remembering. *At least Mum seems to have forgiven me*, I thought.

Turning the corner up Grammar School Lane, I froze and my heart skipped a beat. *Oh no   ... what do I do now?* I thought, as I slowly began to climb the bank. There was no way of avoiding him. I could not turn back but I could not believe it.

Standing at the school gates was the man I had hoped I would never see again. It was him. The same blue boiler suit, the same balding head, and he was looking straight at me.

Maybe he won't recognise me in my uniform, I thought, as I walked towards the gates.

It was not to be. On that first day, and on every school day for the next seven years, Bob the caretaker reminded me of my brief encounter with crime as he greeted me each morning with the words, 'Good morning, Miss Pea,' and smiled knowingly.

My brand-new uniform was at least one size too big, with the blazer sleeves swallowing my hands completely and the skirt, kept up with an old belt, hanging way down past my knees. All the first-year pupils, or 'sprogs' as we were called, paraded around school looking as if we had shrunk overnight. From the first day, I chose to sit at the back of the classroom hoping to go unnoticed. Struggling to see what each teacher was scribbling on the board, I came to the conclusion I needed glasses and raised it with Mum.

'I think I need glasses. I can't see the blackboard at school.'

'Rubbish,' she said, and that was that.

Apart from that initial setback which was eventually resolved, I settled into school and clicked straight away with a girl even smaller than me, called Pauline. She was funny, she was kind and lived a world away from school, high up on the North Yorkshire moors. In winter, the children who hailed from her neck of the woods were often absent due to drifting snow and impassable roads which meant the school bus was cancelled. After much parental discussion, Pauline moved into our house from January to March each year and went home at the weekends. Now that there was an onlooker in her midst, Mum's sharp tongue and cruel hand ceased completely and life at home blossomed.

Each evening after school, homework came first, but after that Mum allowed us comparative freedom. We became world-class acrobats, practising our contortions and taking turns in balancing on top of each other on the lino in the kitchen. On Thursday evenings, we watched *Top of the Pops* and imagined we were Babs and Cherry from Pan's People as we flung our bodies all over the lounge. In bed, we tickled each other's feet and made up stories together. Life was good, we became inseparable and at last I had someone to relate to.

Then things went wrong. In the first few weeks of school, two sixth-form boys called Peter and Bill caught our eye, and we concocted a plan to get them to notice us. How on earth we thought this plan was a winner is beyond me now but it took a whole evening and a lot of deception to develop. Pauline and I sneaked down to the shop and rifled two paper sweet bags before racing back upstairs to our kitchen. Mum was out and Dad was half asleep in the lounge, watching television. Muffling our giggles, we set about coating a 'quarter' of bath bubble balls with toothpaste and quickly rolled each of them in icing sugar. Once dry, we transferred them to the two paper bags, twirled the tops over and hid them deep in our haversacks, ready to accost Peter and Bill the following day. It was their turn as prefects to carry out yard duty and we soon spotted them chatting together on the steps to the dining hall.

'There they are,' I said to Pauline, 'are you ready?'

She nodded and we each pulled out a bag full of 'bonbons' from our blazer pocket as we walked towards them. Timing was critical. If one of them bit into the 'bonbon' seconds before the other, our plan would be ruined.

Wearing the most innocent of expressions, we each held out our bag and smiled sweetly.

'Would you like a bonbon? They're really nice,' I said.

Peter looked at Bill, and Bill looked back at Peter, both knowing that sweets were forbidden at school, but the temptation was too great. Their hands disappeared into separate bags, retrieving two bonbons each, and simultaneously they flung them into their mouths, smiling back at us. As they bit into their bonbons, their smiles turned to confusion – followed by outright rage and embarrassment at being duped.

Peter reacted first, with a wild look in his eyes and managed to roar, 'Detention! Both of you. Report to me after school.'

We did not hang around to see the froth forming around their lips but getting detention devastated us, as we knew our parents would be informed. So much for having a bit of fun.

Dad saw the funny side, but Mum's face erupted when she found out and both of us were punished and our freedom curtailed for a week.

As the months at school went by, two more girls joined our gang and offered us a wider outlook on life. Helena and Ann both lived in a village called Hutton Rudby, close to the Cleveland Hills. Once a week after school, we would grab their school bus and go for tea before shooting off to the village youth club and staying the night in one of their houses.

Hitting thirteen, we huddled together in Ann's bedroom one evening and devised a list for future use, in case the hitherto unthinkable male species ever approached us and we needed to talk in code. We named it the 'How Far Did You Go?' list and, when it came into use, it saved us the embarrassment of having to say the words out loud to each other.

How Far Did You Go?
1. Looking at each other.
2. Smiling at each other.
3. Being asked out.

4. Going out together.
5. Holding hands.
6. The Kiss.
7. The Snog.
8. The Feel.
9. Heavy Petting.
10. Doing It.

None of us believed we would ever reach number ten and have to ask each other afterwards, 'Well … did you *do it*? Did you get to *ten*?'

'Number Ten' still disgusted us slightly, and we were unsure what numbers eight and nine actually meant, but we were armed and ready. For a couple of years, we reported back in numerical code with the highest score from any of us being 'Number Seven'.

'Nose juice soup,' said Dad, when Helena and I asked him what he was boiling in the cauldron look-a-like pot, sitting sturdily on the coal fire range at Burton's Cottage in Staithes.

'Errrggh,' we both shouted, pulling a face, and the two of us collapsed on the settee in a fit of giggles. Mum looked at Dad in disbelief wondering how he could be so crude, but we adored his sense of fun. He sat beside us, his nose streaming, and we all focused on the bubbling cauldron filled with his large, white, cotton hankies.

'I've put them in there to rid them of snot,' he said, leering at us comically.

'That's enough, Sandy,' Mum said, and she turned away busying herself in the kitchen at the other end of the lounge overlooking the harbour.

Burton's Cottage, Staithes - marked with a red dot.

It was the last day of our summer stay at Staithes and Mum granted Helena and me an extra hour around the village, before bedtime.

'Put your anoraks on, it's cold out there,' Mum said as we tried to sidle out unnoticed.

We raced down the 103 stone steps back to the staith, excited to continue our 'jumping off the staith onto the beach and back up the steps' game. On our final attempt before going back to the cottage, disaster struck.

I willed Helena to jump with the words, 'Let's try and break our record and get even further this time. Do you think we can do it?'

She nodded. We gritted our teeth, smiled at each other and with a look of determination launched ourselves off the staith, through the air and onto the sandy beach with a thud.

'Ow,' Helena screamed, and as I raced towards her blood started oozing from her right cheek and all around her eye.

Panic set in. 'What have you done? Here, let me look.'

Beneath the blood, a zip mark was gauged into her cheek, the skin above her eye was cut and she began to cry.

'We'd better go back,' I said as I took her arm and guided her gently off the beach.

Slowly making our way back up the steps to the cottage, Helena's face was as white as a sheet, and she was trembling with shock as blood dripped all down her pale blue anorak.

'My knee went straight in my eye as I landed,' she said, remembering. We both knew we would be in trouble for playing with danger but there was no way out. We had to go back.

Mum, for once, gave me no grief and without a word set about cleaning the wounded warrior. Leaving Dad to deal with his cold and look after Helena, Mum and I made our way back down the steps to the phone box in the middle of the village, to inform the Barkers of their daughter's brush with death. Helena soon rallied, and as the cut on her cheek healed it became the most impressive zip-shaped scab which turned into a scar that lasted for years.

Back at school, December loomed and the importance of the 'How Far Did You Go?' list hit home, as Pauline, Helena, Ann and I began to think that boys weren't so bad after all. 'Number One' kicked in as we looked at them in a different light, followed closely by 'Numbers Two and Three', in my case.

A tiny, blond-haired boy called Tim, reminiscent of the character in *A Christmas Carol,* but without the crutches, smiled at me every time our eyes met in class, and it was not long before he suggested a date.

'Can I take you out, please?' he asked politely, and I agreed. Images filled my head of a romantic walk through the park or sitting in the back row of the movies. Our first and last date was an unexpected venue and freezing cold. He paid for our bus ride to a local train station, where we spent four hours sitting on the side of the platform, notebooks in hand, jotting down the train numbers and nervously chatting. No physical contact, no romance and certainly no thoughts of 'Number Six – The Kiss'.

I liked Tim but not 'in that way' and it was sad to see the disappointment in his eyes as I skirted round the offer of another date, saying, 'Can we leave it for a while, and I'll see.' The coward's way out, I know, but as a shy thirteen-year-old, I was unsure what to say. We remained friends for years after that but the disappointment that our relationship was never more than pure friendship still showed in his eyes.

Romance, however, was on the way for me and the timing could not have been worse.

('Shapes of Things' – The Yardbirds – 1966)

('Georgy Girl' – The Seekers – 1967)

('I Can See for Miles' – The Who – 1967)

11

Disco Dancing

To me, the word 'disco' meant brightly coloured flashing lights, excessively loud music and dancing my heart out until I was exhausted. In my short life, I had only experienced this 'disco' thing while joining in with *Top of the Pops* on a Thursday evening when Mum was out climbing her social ladder. Dad, relaxing on the settee, smiled at me cavorting around the lounge and laughed out loud at my silly contortions as I danced along with Pan's People.

Three months after I turned fourteen, a boy at school in the class above me – known as Noo – asked me to go to my first real-life disco in the church hall in Yarm. A disco in West Street, the street which had always featured highly in my life.

I took the invitation ever so seriously and two weeks beforehand, I got the bus to Stockton. With my pocket money in hand, I scoured the weekend market for disco dress material and a disco pattern. Once back home, I retired to the dining room and started sewing in earnest, singing along to Radio 1 with its disco-style songs.

Practising on our old treadle sewing machine was a task in itself, but I soon learned to keep the wheel turning evenly with my feet pushing back and forth and increased my speed as I practised on an old white sheet. After all, this was my first disco and the thought of my homemade dress falling to pieces while attempting to do 'The Shake' was not part of my plan. I had chosen a fluorescent-orange cotton fabric covered in purple and red flowers which amazingly met with approval from Mum – but only because the pattern was for a neat kind of dress. It had six vertical panels which would help it to swing as I danced, and a very tidy-looking white Peter Pan collar and cuffs. She offered to pin up the hem when I got to that stage and I knew it was to control the finished length and make sure it was not too short. Still, I was so excited at the thought of making my first dress for my first disco and began pinning the pattern on and cutting it all out with vigour.

Three days after, I came home from school to the news that my dad's heart was not enjoying the same even pace as our sewing machine, and it made me even more determined to carry on and complete my work of art to show him.

Dad had suffered a heart attack and had been taken away on a stretcher to North Tees, our local hospital. My mouth fell open when Mum announced I was too young to visit and I walked away in disbelief, taking sanctuary in my room. Immediately my thoughts kicked in,

I'm not too young. I'm fourteen! Why is she doing this?

I reached for my trowel, finished the foundations and flung the first course of bricks onto *The Wall Against Mum.*

While Mum visited Dad, I hammered that treadle machine, sewing like crazy to take my mind off the fact that the person I treasured most in the whole world was so ill and was being kept from me. As the week progressed, Dad improved and eventually came home.

'Can I go and see him?' I asked Mum on returning from school.

'Let him rest, Anne. He doesn't need you disturbing him. He's much better than he was, and you'll see him soon … anyway, you must have homework to do.'

On the Saturday morning after Dad came home, Mum declared that I needed a new pair of shoes for the disco.

Disco? Disco? Do you think I feel like dancing? All I wanted to do was sit with my dad.

'Can I go and see him?' I said, pushing my unwanted toast around.

'No, Anne. He needs to rest and he doesn't need a silly girl like you talking to him all the time.'

For the first time in my life, I pleaded with her saying, 'Please, Mum. I won't say a word. I'll just hold his hand.' A look of what I saw as jealousy swept briefly across her face and permission was denied.

I hate you, I thought, *I really hate you* and went back to laying bricks in my head.

Mum went down to the shop and, wiping my eyes, I put the finishing touches to my disco dress so that I could show my dad. My ears were cocked in case I heard him utter any kind of sound that meant he needed me. Sitting silently on the stairs and listening all the while, I sewed up the hem which Mum had indeed made sure was of an appropriate length. Once finished, I flung it on, and zipping it up I flew up the stairs to show my dad.

'Dad,' was all I dare whisper, as I rounded the corner of his bed wondering if he was awake or asleep. His eyes opened as I took hold of his hand and he smiled that familiar smile, looking me up and down.

'Well done, Tish. It's lovely.' His eyes closed again and, planting a gentle kiss on his forehead, I left the room trying to swallow the most enormous lump in my throat.

'Get better soon, Dad,' I mouthed and went to get changed.

Sally – another of my friends from school – arrived, and reluctantly I got the bus to Stockton with her to look around the shoe shops. Before leaving, we both crept in to see my dad lying there as white as a sheet.

'I'll be back before you know it,' I whispered as I leaned over him giving him a gentle hug. Something told me he was still so very ill and the ache in my throat returned as we crept out of the room.

I knew I had to get shoes as Mum had instructed, and at fourteen my lifelong passion for shoes had well and truly begun, but that day I picked the first pair that fit. A pair of shiny black patent-leather shoes with a daringly high heel, all of one inch. I waited patiently for Sally to find her dream buy. We met prospective disco-goers from school prancing along Stockton High Street, all tremendously excited about the evening's entertainment to come.

I just wanted to get home to my dad. Eventually, and it seemed like a lifetime, Sally found the shoes she wanted, the Yarm bus appeared, and we got on bound for home.

I bypassed Mum in the shop, asked Sally to make herself a drink and flew up the four flights of stairs to see my dad who was still in the same position lying on his back. A weak smile formed, and he stared at me for ages without speaking. I knew what he was thinking. I was his little girl. I was his perfect daughter. I stayed with him as long as I dared and then went down to make lunch for us all.

Eating our sandwiches, I tried to persuade Mum to let me cancel my plans, but she would not listen.

'It'll take your mind off things. Anyway, you've made arrangements, Anne, so that's the end of it.'

Sally and I ate our lunch in silence as neither of us knew what to say to her.

Noo rang our house to confirm that he and his friends would drop by to get Sally and me. Although I wanted to scream out loud that I could not go, I agreed to be ready by half past six.

In the afternoon, Doctor Fraser called to see Dad and announced that he could get up, then off he went on his rounds. What joy I felt. Dad was on the mend.

Sally and I got dolled up for the disco and we looked very grown-up I have to say, with our faces all 'pan-sticked', smudgy-brown eye make-up topped off with mascara and light-coloured lips as a matter of choice. Taking a long look in the mirror and doing a twirl in my new dress and shoes, I was ready for my first ever disco … and I just wanted it to go away.

Going down to the kitchen we heard Mum say, 'I'm getting your Dad up. He wants to see how you look before you go.'

Within seconds, Sally and I heard Dad being sick and it went on and on. Mum screamed from the top of the landing, 'Anne, get the phone book and ring for Doctor Fraser.'

Explaining what had happened, I put the receiver down and stood shaking like a leaf; Sally stood next to me, neither of us knowing what to do. I knew the front door was unlocked as usual, but I flew downstairs to make sure and hovered there waiting for him. When he came, he nodded once and walked straight past me. I followed him upstairs but the bedroom door was closed in my face. Before I could take it all in, he was racing back downstairs into our lounge to ring for an ambulance.

After giving our address, I heard him say the words 'massive coronary thrombosis'. Even though those words meant nothing to me, time stood still, and I knew I was going to lose my dad.

In the midst of all this, the doorbell rang. Being the only people uninvolved, Sally and I ran down to see Noo, all dressed up and ready for action, standing on the doorstep along with other friends from school. The reek of aftershave made my stomach heave and their excited babble fell on deaf ears.

How can I go? I thought, *my dad might need me.* I knew I certainly needed him.

Quietly I announced, 'I'm not coming. My dad's poorly,' and stood frozen to the spot. I looked at Noo and somehow added, 'I'm sorry.'

They all took one look at me and understood it was serious. After a few comforting words, they left along with Sally to explore their new world at the disco. Noo held back and shyly put his arm around me. I glanced at him, all dressed up in his paisley shirt, brown cord jacket and big blue eyes full of concern. I quietly asked him to leave, realising that neither he nor the disco held any interest for me at that particular moment in my life. I just wanted my dad to get better.

Closing the door, I heard movement above and rushed to see what was happening. My dad was slumped in a wheelchair with a face as grey as a November day. He was being wheeled along our first-floor landing towards the stairs. Two ambulance men carried him down to the ground floor. Bundled up in his woolly dressing gown, thick pyjamas and a hospital blanket around his shoulders, I was shocked to see that my dad, my Tosh, was shivering violently. Mum followed as the two men wheeled him to our front door.

My dear dad beckoned me and uttered a single sentence that pierces my heart every time I think of it. I gently cuddled him and, as I stepped back, he looked beyond my eyes and into my soul, gripped my hands with the little strength he had left and said, 'Say "bye-bye" to me, pet.'

I stood there stunned and horrified, for I knew what he was saying. I slowly shook my head, with my eyes locked onto his, refusing to do as he asked. 'I don't need to say goodbye, Dad. You'll be back soon.'

He smiled at me and kept hold of my hand until they took him away. Tosh disappeared in a flash of blue lights and I stood at the front door, shocked and immobile, watching the ambulance speed along the High Street and disappear round the corner over the bridge. I heard its siren becoming fainter and fainter, just like my dad's heart.

Mum doled out her instructions about locking the front door and left in the ambulance with him, leaving me alone in our huge house – as alone as I had ever felt in my young life so far.

I never said goodbye.

Soon, Auntie Freda, one of Mum's sisters, came bustling in and tried to comfort me with various offerings of food, but I refused. We sat in silence pretending to watch the television and waiting for our telephone to interrupt the programme that neither of us was watching.

I stayed up an hour and a half later than usual, waiting for news of Dad.

Mum rang to say he was stable and asked Auntie Freda to sleep overnight.

Safely in bed I may have been, but the strangest thoughts kept me awake for ages. I was giving Mum and Dad points out of ten. I was deciding which one I wanted to die first. I was lying there in the belief that I could control who did. With the points out of ten awarded, I must have gone to sleep.

Somewhere in the distance the following morning, I heard my bedroom door being opened. I turned over to see Auntie Freda walking towards my bed. My first question was the only question I needed an answer to, and the answer was not the one I wanted to hear.

Cold shudders ran through my body as I asked her when Dad was coming home. She stroked my forehead and whispered, 'I'm so sorry pet, but your dad won't be coming home …'

I looked at her in disbelief, willing her to add the word 'yet', but it didn't come. She sat there in silence holding my hand, allowing me to take in what her words meant.

During the night, my dad, the only person I had ever loved, suffered another massive coronary thrombosis and, at the age of fifty-seven, had gone to extend his chain of grocer's shops – this time in heaven.

I shed no tears. I was way beyond that kind of sadness and Auntie Freda asked me to get ready and wait for Mum's return.

My thoughts turned to her. The Mum I didn't belong to, the Mum I was afraid of and the person I disliked more each day. I hated her for keeping me away from Dad, for letting the ambulance men take him away and for always wanting everything done her way. In fact, anything that went wrong from now on, it was sure to be Mum's fault. There was no one else to blame for this. She had nagged him and pushed him to his physical limit, and I would never forgive her for that. It was all her fault.

Memories of Mum's return from the hospital evade me as I blocked the torture of Dad's death from my mind, trying to cope with the pain, the hurt and the grief. Yet I could not shed a tear. I withdrew into a stunned silence.

While Mum arranged my dad's funeral, I sat alone in my room looking out onto the High Street and trying to think positive thoughts. At least I would be able to say goodbye to my dad on the day of the funeral, even if he was not next to me like our 'sing-song-in-chapel' days together. I had never been to a funeral and did not know what to expect and what would be expected of me. What I did *not* expect was Mum saying that I could not attend. She had already decided that I would stay at home along with a couple of relatives, to prepare food and cups of tea for the mourners on their return. There was no discussion and certainly no point in pleading with her. She had made her decision and I had no choice. This was the Mum I was to be up against for the foreseeable future. At the age of fourteen, I was once again deemed too young to be given the chance of coping with real life. In stopping me from going to the funeral, Mum took away my chance of ever being able to say goodbye to my dad.

How utterly cruel you are, I thought. I could not bear to look at her as she spouted forth with the funeral arrangements.

'Do you understand what you've got to do on the day?' she asked.

I slowly nodded my downturned head, filed away a gargantuan piece of resentment into my memory bank and launched a double course of bricks onto the ever-growing *Wall Against Mum*. From that day on, it was impossible to see over the wall. The protective shield I had constructed over the years was obliterating the view.

('Bad Moon Rising' – Creedence Clearwater Revival – 1969)

('Spirit in the Sky' – Norman Greenbaum – 1969)

('Big Yellow Taxi' – Joni Mitchell – 1970)

12

The Death of Tosh

(*'Excerpt from a Teenage Opera'* – Keith West – 1967)

If you are not familiar with the song, please search for it on *YouTube*. Sit back and listen, take in the lyrics and imagine the pain and devastation on that dreadful day when my dear dad departed from the world. Fifty-three years on and the ache in my throat instantly returns whenever I hear this song and memories of Dad fill my head as if it were yesterday. Listen carefully and then walk away without a tear if you can.

Tosh had gone. Tosh was never coming back. I was heartbroken yet I could not cry a single tear. Mum told me that we had to be strong and carry on, as that is what Dad would have wanted. So be it. I would be strong and I would not cry. Sitting on my bedroom window seat and looking towards heaven, I chose a face-shaped cloud to keep my dad close and said goodbye to it, dry-eyed, over and over again. Each day after school, I chose a different cloud and it became 'Dad's cloud'. When life became too much to bear, I spoke to his cloud and shared my innermost thoughts. I asked the cloud how to lessen the grief that was consuming me, how to concentrate at school and how to deal with Mum who was burying herself in the shop and going out in the evenings with her stiff upper lip, leaving me alone. I was a confused and broken fourteen-year-old and I could not believe my dad had gone.

In Mum's defence, she was out at prestigious gatherings and not down the local pub. She had successfully climbed to the top rung of her social ladder and was president of the Women's Institute in Yarm, chairwoman of Yarm Flower Club and an avid bridge player. Being involved in all these gatherings allowed her to chat to friends, old and new, and they supported her through her loss. I was angry that she had moved on instead of grieving for Dad and I still blamed her for his death. I was angry with God for taking such a good man, and the belief Dad had instilled in me through all those years of going to chapel with him, that there was this thing called God watching over us, disappeared overnight.

I only had 'Dad's cloud' and the television to support me. Who could I turn to on a cloudless night when there was nothing on the television? The trauma of losing my dad was scrambling my mind and turning it into a labyrinth of confused thoughts. I needed love from somewhere and Mum was never around long enough to spot the total collapse of Anne, the adopted one. I tried so hard to concentrate on my schoolwork but it was insignificant and worthless. All I could focus on was that Dad had gone and I never got to say goodbye. Mum had snatched the chance of any closure away from me by denying permission to attend his funeral. Night after night, I sat in my room, head in my hands, and whispered, 'Please come back. I need you, Dad. I'm so sorry I didn't say goodbye.' Still the tears refused to come. I would sit on my window seat and search for 'Dad's cloud' and follow it with my eyes until it disappeared from view. The emptiness I felt was unbearable.

He was the only person in the world who had ever completely owned my heart and I thought he would always be there to shelter and protect me. Part of me still believed that one day he would walk back into my life because I had not said that final word to him. Mum never mentioned him and that made his death even harder to bear. Only once did I ask her why, to which she abruptly replied, 'Talking about him won't bring him back, Anne. You need to be strong and move on.'

Each time I searched for 'Dad's cloud', I felt so alone. I needed a cuddle. I needed eyes that held warmth and found me worthwhile. Someone to love me for who I was and not for who I was supposed to be. And there was no one there …

I took to meeting up with friends on school nights while Mum was out because the silence in our house was overwhelming. We congregated on the cobbles outside Danby's ice-cream parlour.

Danby's ice-cream parlour - now Lucy Pittaway's art gallery
(Dave Dowson Photography).

Danby's had evolved into a place to 'hang out' – if you could afford to venture inside. Sitting in the dimly lit café at the back of the shop, the older teenagers ordered frothy Italian coffees, courtesy of the new-fangled, shiny-looking silver machine and watched wide-eyed as it hissed and gurgled preparing their drink.

It all looked so exciting in there, but we were relegated to the cobbles having no money to speak of. I stood there listening to other girls talking about music, make-up and boys but hardly ever joined in. I had nothing to say. I was empty.

The weeks went by, and my friends and I broadened our horizons becoming members of All Saints Youth Club in Eaglescliffe, only a bus ride away. We took on the boys from 'The Comp' at the pool table, listened to music on the jukebox while drinking cheap coffee in the café upstairs and decided that boys were not so bad after all. Some of them were dishy so we practised looking cool and pouting our lips like the 'inside crowd' at Danby's. My heart was elsewhere, however, as the grief of losing my dad followed me like a shadow and battered me every waking hour. After getting back home, I let myself into our huge empty house in Yarm and the grief followed me.

Maybe Mum *did* notice I had reached rock bottom and my schoolwork was plummeting too, but there were no arms to comfort me and no one to tell me it would all be alright in the end.

Out of the blue, she announced a party to 'cheer you up' as she put it. 'I'll borrow a camping stove to put in the yard and we'll have baked potatoes and beans. You can invite who you want but be sensible about it.'

She had obviously thought the whole thing through, and added that if it was raining I could hold the party in the 'other side' of our enormous house as it was now empty. The Best family had left in a huff, weeks after Dad died, disagreeing with Mum's proposed rent increase. Simon Best had left the building and not before time.

In his final weeks of living next door, Simon spent his time trying to coax me to look through the keyhole of the locked dividing door between my bedroom and their second-floor landing. He must have hung around for hours, lying in wait for me to go into my room. As soon as I closed my door, the voice through the keyhole sprang into action with lewd suggestions and requests, and when I lay in bed at night all I could hear was his voice, whispering, 'Psst … Anne … Anne … Anne …'

I stuffed scraps of torn-up newspaper into the keyhole only to find it gone the next day, prised out from the 'other side'. Much to Mum's surprise, and without her say-so, I moved all my furniture around placing my worn-out sofa against that offending keyhole and blocking Simon's view. The voice continued and my bedroom was awash with emotions that constantly clutched at my heart like a tidal wave pulling me under.

Simon added to the emotions racing around my room and I hated him for that. Trying to cope with losing my dad at fourteen years old, I certainly did not need Simon Best preying on me from the 'other side'.

I felt scared.

I felt anxious … and most of all I wanted him to stop. Time after time the hushed requests came through the keyhole and time after time I declined them by remaining silent and still.

'I'll push half a crown under the door if you look at my willy.'

'Let me see your boobs and I'll pay you.'

It was awful. I was in my own bedroom and no one else had a clue what was happening. Who could I go to for help? I was being invaded and made to feel unsafe in the room that had been my sanctuary. Before, I had just felt lonely. Now, I felt unsafe.

I knew I had to do something. I had taken to sitting on the bedroom floor with my back pressed against the only wall that was out of view of the keyhole. Even though the sofa was blocking his view, I believed he was watching and dared not move around my room.

At last, I thought of a solution that could work. The following night, the voice was there again.

'I'll push half a crown under the door if you look at my willy.'

I could almost imagine the shock on his pink-cheeked face, when, after weeks of silence, I answered from 'our side' of the keyhole.

'Yes … alright … I'll look if you promise to stop.'

'Alright, I promise.'

A few minutes passed and I heard Simon whisper, 'Anne, are you looking?'

'Yes,' I answered.

'What can you see then?'

'Your willy.'

The half-crown appeared under the door and a feeling of triumph surrounded me. I grabbed it and rammed it into the back pocket of my jeans, moving away from the keyhole. Throughout our conversation, my eyes had been screwed shut and Simon Best had fallen for my trick. Touché. I had won the battle that had raged for years: Anne versus Simon. I kept that half-crown as evidence and the voice was never heard again.

The word 'party' rang in my ears like the word 'disco' had when Dad was so poorly, but Mum rattled on and it was plain to see the party was going ahead.

The rattling continued.

Mr Frank, from the farm, would be bringing bales of hay for us to sit on, to create 'a proper camping atmosphere' to go with the baked potatoes and beans. Mum agreed I could bring the old HMV record player – which had been my dad's pride and joy – down into the back warehouse and ask everyone to bring 'singles' to play on it.

At the youth club the following week, news of the party spread fast as I made sure everyone knew they were welcome. That included asking boys older than me and who still went to the youth club, even though they had left school at fourteen and had full-time jobs. How grown-up was that? Some smoked, some were in a band and all had wonderfully different clothes and long, flowing hair.

For the first time since Dad died, happy thoughts surrounded me as I lay in bed, hoping the 'Big Boys' would come to the party, even though I was sure they would not. It would be far too babyish an event for them.

Setting up Dad's record player, I was overcome with sadness once more, knowing that I would never hear his wonderful voice again. My throat began to ache, my lips quivered and the tears finally began to fall. It felt like he was right beside me, watching. I could smell him and wanted to snuggle into his shirt, like I had done as a young child hearing the tale of my adoption. I wished with all my heart he could have joined in with my first party without *Musical Chairs* and *Blind Man's Bluff*. I imagined him puffing on his pipe and smiling his smile, silently watching his daughter having a whale of a time. I stood rooted to the spot, surrounded by his presence, shaking and sobbing, and the tears spurted out of my eyes like falling stars.

Pull yourself together, I told myself. *Dad's gone …*

I drifted out into our back yard searching for 'Dad's cloud' to talk to but it was party day and the sky was clear and bright. *And I need to get on*, I thought sadly.

Wait though …

A warm tingle ran down my back as I remembered Dad had been recorded singing with Stockton Stage Society on a proper record and I knew exactly where it was. Now all I had to do was ask Mum's permission to play it while I was setting up for the party.

Convinced the answer would be a resounding 'no', I ran through to the shop, wiping away my tears and trying to control the sharp intake of breath that follows sobbing. When I got there, the words would not come.

'Did you want something, Anne?' she asked, as I started to stutter and stumble through my request. Her fingers quietly drummed on the counter waiting for me to finish, so I took a deep breath, blurted it all out and was amazed by her response. 'Yes, alright, as long as you take it straight back upstairs afterwards. We don't want it getting broken, do we, Anne?' and that was that, conversation over.

With trembling hands, I lowered the needle onto that precious record and drank in my dad's voice as he belted out the songs from *Merry England*, *The Mikado* and *HMS Pinafore*. I knew them all off by heart.

Dad's magnificent voice lives on to this day.

I sang through my tears at the top of my voice as I had done at chapel with him. I was Dad's songbird, resurrected. I launched into the dance routines imagining I was dressed up in a striped sailor's outfit and danced away my sadness. I was in another world and it instantly confirmed my belief that music would always help me through the bad times.

Looking up as I finished, I spotted Mum watching me from the first-floor kitchen window. Instead of feeling like the shy showgirl of old, I was proud to have been singing Dad's songs and for her to be there watching.

She opened the window and called out, 'Your lunch is ready.'

The party went without a hitch. All my friends came and a few boys from the grammar school too. We had a choice of lemonade, cream soda or orangeade to drink and all from our wonderful shop. Mum was friendly as she always was in company. She watched my friends and me dancing to the music of such groups as The Beatles and The Faces. The boys from school sat on the hay bales fidgeting, unsure what to do or where to look, so we grabbed them by the hand and pulled them up to dance. They danced with their eyes fixed firmly on the floor and we all kept on dancing until Mum asked, smiling, 'Anyone for food?' and we went over to join her.

We began to dish up, when lo and behold, the 'Big Boys' sauntered into the yard through the open garage door that led to the side street. My face began to burn and I could not believe they had come. Mum's smile disappeared and she marched over to interrogate them. I flew after her, pointing out that they were from the youth club and I had asked them to come.

'Well as long as you behave yourselves,' she said to them and they were taken aback by her stern manner, realising that this woman was not to be messed with.

We all stood around eating and Mum stood firm, supervising the whole event until she had finished her plate of food. To my surprise, she then announced that she was 'going in for a while' and added, without a smile, 'I'll be in the kitchen if you need me ... and watch what you're doing.'

Us girls went back to dancing together. The boys from school looked even more uncomfortable than before in the presence of the new arrivals and were back on their hay bales, fidgeting again.

Two of the 'Big Boys' came over and joined in with the dancing. My legs turned to jelly and I could feel myself blushing furiously. Then, one by one, they asked some of my friends to go for a walk by the river.

What was I supposed to say to Mum if she came back down? And why did they want to go to the river anyway?

After about half an hour they all reappeared and the 'Big Boys' sauntered off down the side street. The boys from school left soon after and the party subsided. The girls who had stayed in the yard rushed to question the girls who had gone to the river, using our 'How Far Did You Go?' list and all their answers tallied: 'Number Seven – The Snog.'

Even though we were talking in code, they blushed as they said the number out loud. It was the first time any of them had been 'snogged' and it had happened at my first grown-up party.

After helping Mum to tidy up, we laid face down in a circle in my bedroom, quietly devising another list – and this time it was about the 'Big Boys'. We gave them marks out of ten for three different things: *Looks ... Clothes ... Hair.* Personality did not come into it, as the girls who had gone to the river were too busy being 'snogged' to get to know their respective 'Big Boy'.

One by one my friends were collected, apart from Pauline who stayed the night. Mum collared us and gave us a long lecture about any future contact with the 'Big Boys'.

'With hair like that, they're bound to be up to no good. No more Danby's for you two for a while, and we'll have to see about the youth club.'

She went on to say that they were probably involved in drink and drugs and, as they were older than us, they would expect 'different things' from a girl. They should be left alone to look for someone of their own age. Both of us knew that Mum had made up her mind and there was no point in trying to defend them.

After the party, I kept on thinking of one particular 'Big Boy' and wondering why he had not chosen me to go down to the river for a 'snog'. Not that I could have gone missing anyway, and I would not have known what to do when I got there, having only been kissed once in my life on 'Grassy Bank' at the age of five years old. Still, I was disappointed he had asked Geraldine, my slim, blonde, leggy friend instead of me. I began to wonder what he was called …

In the weeks that followed, Mum reverted to her usual self. Controlling, stony-faced and disappointed in me, no matter how hard I tried to live up to her expectations.

I stuck to the rules and stayed away from Danby's café. I tried hard with my schoolwork but found myself wandering off into the world of memories of my dad. At night, when Mum was out and about, I sat on the lounge window seat watching the world go by in the High Street and telling 'Dad's cloud' how my day had been. My heart constantly ached for him and the party had not fixed that.

Eventually, I returned to the youth club after I had reassured Mum that my friends and I would avoid the 'Big Boys' if they happened to be there. Sometimes they came sauntering in, gave us a passing glance and quickly moved on.

Danby's café came back into play when we were all a little older. Some of us had Saturday jobs by then and could occasionally afford to join the 'inside crowd' for one of those frothy foreign coffees or something as silky-tasting as a strawberry milk shake.

'Not such a rebel,' I hear you say. Well, that's because I was toeing the line and trying to be the perfect daughter. Abiding by the rules. Mum's rules. For a while anyway …

('Days' – The Kinks – 1968)

('The Boxer' – Simon and Garfunkel – 1969)

In Loving Memory of Tosh (1912-1969)

Grey-faced, from your wheelchair

You tried to grip my hand

Say goodbye, pet, say goodbye

Those words I could not stand.

No, Dad, no I can't

I can't say goodbye

How was I to know right then

You were going away to die?

You were my treasure, my Tosh

How could I look at you and believe

That this moment would be the end of time?

Although you knew you had to leave.

Parents are immortal

Or so the children think

And somehow I believed that

Until you crossed the brink.

Forever after that

Every sunrise would mean

A heart full of pain and sorrow

And another waking dream ...

...of looking skywards

For one long lost face

And every day I found it

I saw you and I traced ...

...your face shape in a cloud

And talked to it and asked out loud

'Why did you go, Dad?

Why did you leave?'

I needed you

I loved you so

And because I did not get to say goodbye

I could not even grieve.

Written with love for Tosh, by Tish – 1984

('Fire and Rain' – James Taylor – 1970)

13

The Summer of '69

Hinton's, the first self-service supermarket in Yarm, opened its doors while Dad was still alive, and on reflection I realise that was another nail in his coffin – and that of our shop. I applied for a Saturday job there to distance myself from Mum at the weekends and earn money too. I was unaware of the impact on our family of Hinton's opening up but, on announcing my new job, Mum raised the roof completely and forbade it without giving any reason. I tackled her, for the first time in my life, and Dad stepped in too.

Laying his hand on her arm to calm her down, he said, 'Just let her go, Madge.'

Mum flinched, glared at him and walked away.

Each Saturday, I finished my shift walking out with a pound note stuffed in my overall pocket and I felt like a millionaire. My job lasted less than a year as school stepped in after I was chosen for both the hockey and tennis teams. Mrs Honeyman, my PE teacher, made it clear that playing for the school at weekends was expected as a commitment to school life.

How can she control my weekends? I thought, but no one dared to disagree with Mrs Honeyman. As a customer, Mum and Dad knew her well. As a teacher, with a face that said 'you will do as I say', I had no choice. Instead of a Saturday job, I worked in the school holidays and was proud to get my pay packet at the end of each week. Even better was the praise I got for being a hard worker. That made me shine inside and stand tall, although I found it hard to accept or believe and was unsure how to respond.

My favourite holiday job was helping to run a summer playscheme at *The Links*, one of the local primary schools in Eaglescliffe. Children between three and eleven years old came bounding in like puppies each day, wondering what was in store. Weather permitting, we arranged outside activities on the playing fields overlooking the River Tees. On wet days, the children painted and drew, sang songs while pummelling clay, or put on shows, bossily choreographed by the older children dragging the younger ones into their positions ready for action.

My recollection of the summer of '69 is of happy children bouncing around and chattering non-stop unless they were focused on the quieter activities. Every child relished every session, and they were all shattered and ready to wind down by the end of the day, congregating on coloured cushions in the corridor. One of their favourite games was I Spy and I can still picture the animated face of a blonde, curly-haired six-year-old turning red with frustration and frantically waving her hands in the air, waiting to answer. The word exploded from her mouth when she was picked and it was 'correct' so now it was her turn to say,

'I Spy, with my little eye, something beginning with … "S".

'S' came out as 'F'. We started searching. She became even more frustrated than before with our suggestions, including 'floor', 'foot' and 'face'.

Scowling at us she said, '*No*, I said "S"!' (which still came out as 'F').

Eventually, I had the bright idea of asking her if she meant 'S' and drew the letter on the board. She looked at me as if I was mad and shouted,

'Yef, fat'f what I faid ifn't it!' – turning even redder with all the effort this had taken. Now that we understood we were looking for something beginning with 'S', our eyes scoured the room and we gave our suggestions.

None were 'correct'.

'Shall we give in?' I asked everybody. Tired and hot and ready to go home, they all nodded their heads. Our curly-haired six-year-old rose to her feet, puffed out her chest and, with a beaming smile, pointed upwards and shouted,

'Ceiling!'

Well, that was it. Everyone fell about giggling and telling her how cute she was. She looked at them all and carried on beaming, believing that she had beaten us all into submission at the end of another happy day.

By the time I finished there in that wonderful summer of '69, I began to think that working with children was a good option for the future. It was a passing thought as I also fancied training to be a librarian. I had always loved books, especially the peace and quiet needed to read them, and libraries were such calming places to visit. Like my love of music, books offered me an escape from the real world and from Mum.

As something to say at the dinner table one night, I made the mistake of sharing the thought of becoming a teacher. Immediately, Mum latched onto the idea and her face lit up, pleased that I had finally said something sensible. Then she voiced her opinion, 'I'm not sure if you're clever enough to get to college and even if you are, do you think you're good enough to become a teacher?'

Thanks, Mum, I thought, *that gives me so much confidence.* All my life, any of the ideas I shared with her were immediately deflated by her negative response.

'You'll never do that.'

'What a stupid idea.'

And so on.

She would always butt into our conversation by saying, 'Oh Anne, why can't you just get to the point? You've got such a long-winded way of saying things.' *Aka* 'I'm not interested.'

I could see it in her eyes and the way she set her mouth, brushing me to one side whenever I spoke, and according to her I always used the wrong words anyway. She constantly compared my achievements to hers and the only time she was proud of me was when I acted as she would have done. Over the years, I became accustomed to her criticising me and never having faith in my abilities, but it felt awful. It nibbled away at my confidence and talking to anyone began to fill me with dread. I took to planning what to say before I said it, in case my words came out wrong. By the time I had worked out what to say, the moment was over. My self-esteem and confidence plummeted, and I fell silent. I reverted to being 'the listener'.

In the midst of all this, a part of me somehow remained strong and, each time Mum attacked, my overriding thought was, *I'll show you one day.* My inner strength lived on, the part that was bred in my bones, and I clung onto it trying to dismiss the part that she almost succeeded in making me believe. The part that said I was worth nothing.

Mum never gave up on the 'teacher thing' and she soon spread the word. It became the path chosen for me – as had happened all my life. I went off the idea simply because I was being pushed in yet another direction that was not my choice. I had only mentioned it once and purely as an option and a topic of conversation to lighten the silence at the dinner table.

As the '70s decade dawned, Mum worked full-time in our shop trying to make it viable. My role was to come home from school, feed myself and get on with my homework, so I grabbed the same things week after week from the shop shelves. I became plump from all the rot I was eating and was dropped from the hockey and tennis team for a while. Straight away, I looked for another Saturday job and was taken on at Aline's grocery shop next to Danby's. It was a tiny shop run by Aline, a friendly little grey-haired lady, sporting shabby slippers and a grubby white grocer's coat. Her flabby, overweight husband occasionally came to help with his dirty-shirted stomach spilling over his trousers, and all held up by braces. He wore slippers too.

Christine, one of my school friends, worked there with me and each Saturday night we left with a pound note in our pockets.

Back in the millionaire's league again!

At first, I was worried about making mistakes, but I soon got the hang of the job, and my confidence took a timid leap upwards. We were taught the ropes by an older girl called Cynthia who worked there full-time and virtually ran the place. She was patient and kind and her blonde bouffant hairdo intrigued me, all backcombed and grown-up looking like Dusty Springfield. Every Saturday lunchtime after finishing work at 'The Skinyard', her boyfriend Howard stood at the front counter chatting to her while we were waiting for our next customer. He had black hair and long whiskery sideboards like a teddy boy – and a proper twinkle in his dark eyes when he gazed at Cyn, which was his name for her. I knew they would get married one day and I wanted someone of my own to look at me like that. *That would be lovely,* I thought.

One of our regular customers on a Saturday was a professional footballer called Nobby Stiles who played for my favourite team, Middlesbrough or 'The Boro' as we called them. He came into Aline's like clockwork, for one thing and one thing only: a pint of milk. He was a short man and looked nothing like a famous person to me. He was going bald even though he was still young and he combed his remaining hair over the top of his head in a vain attempt to hide his balding patch. He also had false teeth which he took out for each match and, summing him up, I would say that he was not the most attractive footballer in the world, but he always had a smile on his face.

Soon after I started, Cynthia saw Nobby walk in and rushed to serve him. He came up to the counter, smiled with his teeth fully in, and said, 'A pint of milk please.' Only it didn't come out like that. 'A p …p …p …pint of milk please,' was what we heard that day and every Saturday after that.

Poor Nobby. Not only did he have a name like Nobby, was going bald and had false teeth in his twenties, but he also had a stammer. Cynthia stood firm, looking him straight in the eye and did not move a muscle to reach for the milk until after he spluttered out what he wanted. I thought that was so kind, as she knew exactly what he had come for but out of respect held back and let him finish his sentence. We learned to do the same and every time without a smirk or a giggle.

I stood corrected by Mum when I shared the story of Nobby Stiles. On mentioning who he played for, she stopped me in my tracks – telling me that 'The Boro' was not pronounced 'The Burra'. That was the common way to say it. The correct pronunciation was 'The Borrow'. Somehow, I refrained from laughing in her face as for once I *knew* she was wrong. I took it on the chin and remained silent.

Hinton's supermarket continued to thrive but our shop was slowly sliding downhill. Even customers we thought of as friends 'popped into' Hinton's to see what it was like. They still got most of their groceries from us but many of them reported back how much cheaper the prices were along the street at Hinton's. When the hooter sounded for their ten o'clock break, the lads from 'The Skinyard' stopped coming for their snacks and 'Vic the Spiv' spotted them going into Hinton's instead. Some of the farmers' wives who had enjoyed free deliveries from our shop for years, now had more reliable cars and drove into Yarm to shop, at Hinton's. I was so glad that my dad was not there to witness all the traitors sneaking in and out with bags full of provisions.

(*'The Times They Are a-Changin'* – Bob Dylan – *1964*)

~~~

A year after Dad died, Mum announced she would be 'selling up'. *Where will we go?* I wondered. The anger towards Mum that had been festering inside me since Dad's death came flooding back with a vengeance. We were leaving the shop, the only home I had ever known.

Even though it was a cold and lonely place, it had been my home for eleven and a half years. And what's more, we would be leaving my dad behind. Mum would forget the years of slogging he had put into that shop and given his life for, trying to make it work. That I could not bear. I still believed Mum was to blame for my dad's death, with her constant nagging and her high-flying expectations. This was a turning point in my life. Although I knew we had to leave, resentment towards Mum exploded, another course of bricks flew onto *The Wall Against Mum* which was now almost as tall as me, and I transformed myself into a 'Dadless rebel' fighting against the years of control.

In the summer of '69, I spent those warm summer nights standing on the cobbles outside Danby's, all mini-skirted up with one foot turned inwards like Twiggy in an attempt to look cool. My friends and I talked to boys in earnest and I was the shy, quiet one. Some boys offered us cigarettes and the occasional ride out in a car and we accepted both gladly. We were still good girls at heart and did not attach ourselves to anyone in particular but enjoyed the fun of being wild and mischievous. We pushed our luck and occasionally ignored our curfew, but luck was on my side as there was no one at home to check what time I had landed.

Up to now, I have neglected to tell you that, soon after my twelfth birthday, my breasts decided to show the world what was 'bred in the bone'. By the time I was fourteen, they had sprouted, flowered and flourished into a size 34 E, overshadowing my petite frame. They were huge and they hurt. For a whole year after the sprouting began, Mum insisted there was no need for a bra. My back constantly ached and it was hard to sit up straight. I compared these pendulous attachments of mine to other girls at school and mine definitely won the booby prize. The girls with their pretty gingham or flowery bras were relatively flat chested and there I was, hopefully fully-grown but without a bra.

PE lessons were a pure embarrassment. Before each lesson, I hid in the toilets to get changed and caught up with the rest of the girls as they left the changing room, rounding my shoulders to camouflage the size of my breasts. PE lessons were painful too. Running hurt, jumping hurt and I blushed furiously each time I glanced up to see the boys in my class with their eyes glued to my bulging breasts. I hated what was happening to me.

I saved up my pay from Aline's, got the bus to Stockton and bought myself a bra. There were all sorts of colours and styles displayed in the shop but as they neared my size the choice disappeared. I was left with one choice only. White, white or white. They were disgustingly huge and ugly, but I knew I had to have one. Coming home on the bus after my first professional fitting, the support offered was amazing. With my shoulders back and the pain almost gone, I sat there and wondered why Mum had denied me that comfort.

One Friday after school in the summer of '69, Pauline came to stay. Mum was out as usual, this time playing bridge. With our homework finished, we dolled ourselves up and raced over to the cobbles outside Danby's.

The 'Big Boys' came strutting down the High Street and nonchalantly hung around for a while. Two of them, called Bert and Keith, came over to chat. We were flattered that they preferred talking to us rather than going off to do the things 'Big Boys' could get away with on a Friday night. Maybe it was because we offered them a cigarette that we had sneaked from our shop or because they could see the size of my breasts. Or maybe it was because they liked talking to us. For whatever reason, Bert and Keith had shown an interest. Pauline and I glanced at each other in shock as they strutted off, unable to believe the precious moments we had encountered.

Bert was the 'Big Boy' at my party who had chosen Geraldine to take down to the river for a snog. Since then, I had often pictured him working away in 'The Skinyard' behind our shop, hair tied back in a sandy-blonde ponytail and splodging through the chemicals in his green wellies. I wondered why I kept thinking about him and came to the only conclusion that fitted. I must fancy him. I had never felt like this before and it was such a strange, warm feeling.

A week later, Mum told me that she had accepted an offer on our shop and found a house for us.

'We'll make a new life in Eaglescliffe,' she said. 'We'll be much nearer Auntie Freda.'

I was horrified. Even though Auntie Freda was my favourite auntie, the thought of visiting her and watching her dodgy television screen rolling round and round was not high on my list at fourteen years old. The thought of sucking out the custard from a vanilla slice each Saturday afternoon as a 'treat' from Spark's bakery could not tempt me to feel excited either. I wanted to see Bert again outside Danby's. There was nothing I could do to change things. We were moving. Even though the offer on our shop was ridiculously low, proffered by a posh solicitor in Yarm eager to get into property development, Mum was desperate to get rid of the shop and its memories and had agreed to sell. There was no going back.

The day before we left, I came back from school and my stomach turned over when I spotted that my Royal Enfield bicycle had vanished from the hallway. In disbelief, I flew into the shop to ask Mum where it was and the abrupt answer was a final shot through the heart for me.

'Well, you haven't used it for weeks, have you, Anne? I've given it to the Marsdens. Their children will appreciate it more than you.'

I walked away without a word, pressing my lips together until they were numb, to stop me from screaming at her and possibly launching out. My heart was thumping with the anger I felt towards her. Reaching into my school haversack, I grabbed my trowel and *The Wall Against Mum* shot up in height by another course. Standing on tip-toe, I craned my neck again to try and peer over it but it was no use. I was trapped behind the wall.

I cannot remember moving out of our huge house above the shop. Nor do I remember moving to Eaglescliffe, but on that first night there I woke up dripping with sweat and sobbing my heart out, shouting my dad's name. In my nightmare, I was searching for him and he was nowhere to be seen. When I found him, he walked away into the distance. I ran and ran, screaming his name, but I could not reach him. Then he disappeared again and I woke up sobbing. It took me weeks to sleep properly after that horrendous nightmare. I could not let go and still believed he would walk in with his familiar smile, saying, 'Hello Tish. I've missed you *so* much.'

Mum started her new job a week after we moved, courtesy of Dad's best friend who owned a haulage company in Stockton. I walked the two miles to school and back, five days a week, passing our shop and quietly remembering.

In the weeks that followed I returned to Yarm. Pauline and I met Bert and Keith under cover of the crowd outside Danby's café. As the evenings went by, we distanced ourselves from the rest of the crowd and the two of us started 'going out' with our respective 'Big Boy'. Both Bert and Keith had left 'The Comp' the year before and, after a week of freedom, had been catapulted into the world of full-time work at 'The Skinyard'. To me, it meant the smelly factory behind our shop full of sad memories. Rex, our spaniel, was killed by a wagon driver delivering sheep pelts when I was four years old. Tom Dooley, my cat, fell into what was known as the 'lime pit' and was burned to death by the acid, and Simon Best tied me up outside the factory as part of a game when I was seven and left me for dead.

Things had moved on from those memories, and at the age of fifteen,

'The Skinyard' took on a whole new meaning. It was where my new boyfriend worked six days a week. For the first time in my life I was in love, and I knew Mum would go through the roof if she found out about Bert. In her eyes, everything about him would be unsuitable. He had long hair, he had left school to work in a job that was going nowhere and he played bass guitar in a band. All these things about Bert told me I had to keep this love of my life secret from Mum for a while. In my eyes, he was a grown-up, a kind and loving grown-up, and no one was going to tear us apart. Each time I looked into his beautiful blue eyes, I saw the truth and a special twinkle only for me. In the summer of '69, I knew I had found the love of my life. For the first time since Dad died, I felt alive and knew I belonged to Bert.

Bert, Colin and Keith. Clock the platform boots!

I secretly entered the grown-up world of smoke-filled pubs, alcohol and brightly lit jukeboxes in the favourite haunts of Bert and his music-mad friends. He took me to The Blue Bell on the way into Yarm and The George and Dragon, right in the middle of the High Street. It was wonderful to be back in my hometown. We spent evenings loading up the jukebox and listening to unbelievable musicians like Cream, Jeff Beck and Free in the back room of the George and Dragon. Pauline and I danced underneath the strobe light which made everyone's teeth shine bright white like film stars. Each song held memories in the years to come which cast an ache through my heart.

My shyness and sorrow took a back seat. Bert taught me to laugh again, and I felt secure in his presence. We belonged together. I was introduced to lager and I adored it – or perhaps it was more the effect it had on me. Drinking alcohol allowed me to relax completely and begin to find out who I was. I loved the taste of the new life it gave me, full of confidence, conversation and laughter, and it took me to a place that was probably within me from the start.

The good times did not last for long. Mum found out about Bert, and he was blamed for everything. He was blamed for my schoolwork going downhill. My whole attitude towards her changed completely, and he was blamed. The clothes I wore became more bohemian and Bert was blamed. Poor, dear Bert could do no right in Mum's eyes, and I was told that I could not see him anymore.

'It's forbidden,' was all she said.

I was growing up in front of her eyes if she had bothered to notice, and I could not be controlled, suppressed or humiliated any longer without fighting back. The rebel in me had reared its head.

When she forbade me from seeing Bert, I reached for my trowel and flung some more bricks onto *The Wall Against Mum*.

That kind of command from Mum to a teenager so in love was like a red rag. And to a teenager in the 1960s, and an adopted one at that, it was the signal to start answering back and finally questioning my Mum's authority. A signal to become more devious by sneaking out of the house when she was at her social gatherings and falling into Bert's arms under 'our' tree, then sneaking back in before she came home. It was the signal to invite Bert to our house, only to have him scramble and leap over the six-foot back garden fence at the sound of Mum's Mini pulling up on the drive.

Unbeknown to her, Bert and I continued to see each other whether it was at home, at the youth club or at the pubs in Yarm. We went for idyllic walks whatever the weather and stopped to kiss and express our undying love for each other. Some weeknights we stood under 'our' tree, around the corner from my new house, and we knew that tree would always be our special place. We talked of life and how we would always be together.

We chose to paint our names in white metallic paint above the front bumper of his black Austin Somerset. This was to announce to the world how much we loved each other. *Bert and Anne forever.*

His car became our sanctuary, and we drove into the country to find a secluded spot or lay-by where we could wrap ourselves around each other in our own magic. We went to his parents' house when everyone was out (including his brother Howard, of 'Howard and Cyn' fame) and listened, hand in hand, to LPs crackling as they blasted out their music on the record player. He taught me how to play 'House of the Rising Sun' on his acoustic guitar and once again we ended up showing each other how much we were in love, in a way that parents would most certainly not understand.

Before he came out to meet me, he scrubbed 'The Skinyard's' filthy chemicals off his face but most nights there were hard green bits still stuck to his sandy-blonde hair. I picked them off, grooming him like a monkey, and it was all part of being close. The months sailed by and the deviousness continued. At weekends, I went to Yarm and I must have been so naïve in thinking that Mum did not know I was in the pub with Bert and all our friends. He used to walk me home but veer off at that last bend by 'The Comp' and, holding my head up high, I walked the rest of the way alone.

Sometimes Pauline would stay over and a new routine emerged. Mum would always greet us the next morning with the same three questions:

'Where did you go?'

'Who were you with?'

'What did you do?'

She must have known the answers would be a lie or a truth bent to suit what she wanted to hear, but the questioning continued. She must also have known that Bert was in the picture somewhere but preferred to hear that I was out and about with others.

In between the loving and laughing, the smoking and drinking, I managed to fit in revising for my GCE 'O' levels and came away with five passes out of the eight subjects taken.

When I got my results, Mum simply said sarcastically, 'I knew you wouldn't do well ... I wonder why?'

('House of the Rising Sun' – The Animals – 1964)

('Those Were the Days' – Mary Hopkin – 1968)

('Where Do You Go To My Lovely' – Peter Sarstedt – 1969)

('Take Off Your Clothes' – Peter Sarstedt – 1969)

('Summer of '69' – Bryan Adams – 1985)

14

The Black Box

'Today you are going to create your family tree. Does anyone know what that means?'

Mrs Atkinson, who seemed way past retirement age to me, stood on the lectern at the front of the class with round-rimmed glasses, rouge splodged across her cheeks and her usual carpet slippers, nursing her swollen feet. The words that poured from her mouth floored me completely, and I wanted to bolt from the room. Hands shot up as everyone competed to answer, apart from mine which stayed clamped to the desk, singling me out. All eyes were on me as the whispers reverberated around the classroom.

The echo of one word filled my head and my face flushed with embarrassment as it grew louder.

'Adopted' … 'adopted' … 'adopted' …

Richard Surfleet, the curly-haired 'professor of pupils' and a wonderful friend, took control by interrupting their whispers and answered her question in adult language that none of us had yet fully mastered.

'A family tree is the most common form of visually documenting one's ancestry. It's a type of diagram representing generations of families and how they are linked through the years,' he said and gave me an unnoticed nod. *Oxford, here he comes*, I thought, and nodded back, with a weak smile.

An hour later, our diagrams complete, I sat wondering why the branches on my tree portrayed lie after lie. Even though I had a family to add to my tree, it was not my real family and the whole class was somehow aware of that fact. I had only broken links and knowledge of none of them. There was one way to find out. The 'black box'.

Since Dad had died, Mum instantly shut me down each time I dared to ask anything about my adoption, repeating what she had said all my life during Sunday night bath times, 'I'll explain it when you're older and can understand.'

On each occasion, I turned and walked away to avoid the explosion of my whole being. I was fifteen at the time and definitely old enough to understand. I knew that. She knew that too but for her the subject was awkward to discuss and easier if avoided. Now and again, I gave myself permission to repeat the unwanted questions and Mum shut me down, cut me off and walked away leaving me alone to wonder. 'Dad's cloud' came into play, as I leaned out of my window asking for help. The cloud kept its silence time after time. The ignorance tortured me and the black metal box was my only hope of finding a solution.

The box had known one home in its long life: under their bed at our house in Yarm. Year after year it lay there, and as soon as we moved into our new house it took up its new home under Mum's bed, hidden from view with its secrets intact. I grew up with the importance of the black box, as my parents mentioned it on many occasions when precious papers needed to be retrieved or stored somewhere safe.

'It'll be in the black box,' Dad would say.

'Put it in the box, then we'll know where it is.' An instruction from Mum.

Whenever the box was required, a ceremony followed, as Dad carried it into the room. Prising the lid open, he lifted out papers or put them away. Then the box was gone, back under their bed. As a child, the mystery of the black box intrigued me, and I wondered what secrets lay hidden in there. Putting two and two together as I grew up, I believed there must be something inside that box to do with the secret of my identity, but I was too scared to look … until we moved from Yarm.

Each time Mum left me alone in the evenings in our new house, I crept into her room and sat cross-legged on the carpet between the twin beds, hunching down to get a better view of the black box. My heart raced as I knew I was wrong in even thinking about opening it. Time after time, I gave up and left the room too scared to complete my mission, until one day another bitter argument between Mum and I gave me the right to know. Heaving the box out from under her bed with my heart pounding, I reached for the lid before my courage failed me. I sat there, silent and still, with despair descending. The box was locked.

Why is it locked? I thought. To me, that proved something within it was not for my eyes. It proved what I had believed for years.

The hunt for the key began and my web of deceit spiralled as, each time Mum left me alone at home, I rifled through handbags, pockets and drawers all belonging to her. I was desperate for the truth. Somehow, I expected her to fly in and catch me red-handed, heart pounding and guilty as charged. The key eluded me. Its shape, its size and its whereabouts were all unknown to me and I gave up for a while, distraught. My mission had failed. I shared this with no one apart from 'Dad's cloud'. As usual, the cloud remained silent.

As winter set in, I rummaged through the hall stand drawer to find some gloves to wear for my walk to school. The sound of metal at the back of the drawer took my thoughts straight back to the black box. Listening to Mum clearing up in the kitchen, I grabbed the entire pile of gloves to unveil the source of the sound and spotted what I had been searching for. Almost hidden in the depths of the drawer, lay this rusty old barrel key, looking up at me. An involuntary shudder ran through my body, and I knew my search was over. I had found the key – the key to the black box and hopefully to my true identity. Hastily replacing the pile of gloves, I shouted, 'I'm off now,' and left the house with my head buzzing as thoughts of my next course of action whirled round in my head.

The Key to My Identity.

Two evenings later and with Mum out for hours, I was back in her room holding the key and trembling from head to foot.

Go on, Anne, try it, I told myself, but I could not do it and left her room, replacing the key in the same spot in the hall stand drawer.

Night after night, with my heart pounding, I picked up that key and crept into her room only for my courage to fail me at the last minute. I was not strong enough to go through my mission alone. I sat cross-legged and hunched over for hours just staring at the black box and chewing my nails, willing it to magically open and pour out the information I needed to know. But the lid remained closed.

Just try the key! At least you'll know if it fits.

Down on my haunches, I reached for the box with my heart racing and pulsing through my head. Pulling it towards me, I pushed in the key. Success! The key to my life fit perfectly. Now all I had to do was lift the lid.

There are many times in life when things happen to stop you in your tracks. That night when I slid the key into the lock of the black box, turned it and heard the lid creak as it opened remains number one in my memory bank. The musty smell of ageing paper hit my nostrils as I peered inside and somehow I knew the secret of my identity was held within. I was about to unveil the secret that Mum had chosen to hide from me for fifteen years. History lay in that box. *My* history.

Rifling through, I saw stack upon stack of old brown envelopes. I had no chance of finding what I was looking for.

Don't give up. Lift them out and put them back in the right order, I told myself. The years of deceit I had developed to side-step Mum's control was instructing me to act and cover my back.

With my hands shaking, I carefully lifted them out, one by one. I was aware that time was ticking by and Mum would be home soon. I had no desire to see what the contents of each envelope were unless I spotted something to do with my adoption. The pile of irrelevant envelopes mounted up beside me and my heart sank, believing that the frantic search for the key had not been worth it. There was nothing in the box to offer me a solution to the years of wondering and reflecting upon who I was. My eyes were brimming with tears as I reached for the penultimate envelope and three words on the one underneath, written in my dad's handwriting, leapt out at me.

'Correspondence regarding Anne.'

For a moment I froze, too frightened to continue.

'Correspondence regarding Anne' hidden in the black box.

I stared at it, too stunned to act, and I could not get my breath. My heart was punching against my chest and saliva filled my mouth. Taking deep breaths and ignoring the overwhelming sensation of nausea, I picked up the envelope and shoved my hand in, pulling out the contents.

A shiver engulfed me as I devoured what was inside, digesting it as fast as I could. Old cards from relatives welcoming me into the family, a small, brown pay packet with 'Anne's first tooth' written on the front, and a lock of blonde wavy hair lying at the bottom of another small envelope. I did not have time to study those parts of my past. They would have to wait.

I unfolded a piece of ageing foolscap paper and the words flashed before my eyes, causing the feeling of nausea to rise in my throat once again. Shock surged through me, and in a split second, that piece of paper obliterated the familiar world I had known for fifteen years. An emotional landslide swept me off my feet, churning up my feelings of insecurity, and carried me straight back to the beginning of my life.

An official blue stamp on the adoption order told me that what lay before me was the truth. This was me. I had found myself at last.

The start of the first line read as follows:

IN THE MATTER OF … Pauline Catterson … AN INFANT …

… The name made me jerk backwards and clutching the piece of paper with my face burning, I scanned the rest of the document for further clues. A few lines below, another name leapt out at me and lodged itself deep within my brain. The name became a blur as I reacted to the shock and my whole body went into overdrive, shaking uncontrollably. I tried to focus on the name and said it over and over in my head. Mary Whyte Catterson … Mary Whyte Catterson … Underneath her name, the word 'mother' spelled out her relationship to me and it meant my search for her was over. Or was it just beginning?

I carried on scouring the adoption order for one more name to complete the picture. But it was not there. The space where my father's name should have been typed was filled in with a single dash.

But I must have a father? I thought. *He has to be somewhere.*

Like a flash, I convinced myself that it did not matter to me at that moment. I had found my real name. I had found my mother's name and that would do for now. The jigsaw was coming together after all these years. My eyes flew to the bottom of the document to see my birthplace registered as Scarborough … in the county of York. *So that's why we often used to go there*, I thought. *I wondered why they took me back there again and again.*

Throughout my life, my sixth sense had told me I was of Scottish origin and, in one fell swoop, that part of my identity I had believed in ceased to be. Turning the document over, my date of birth flashed before me and I was elated to see that something had stayed the same. As I sat there taking it all in, my breathing slowed, the shaking subsided but panic set in.

'Put it all back. Put it all back. She'll be home soon,' I whispered to myself, in a voice I did not recognise. Taking one last look at my identity, I replaced the various pieces of paper, with some still unseen, into the 'Correspondence regarding Anne' envelope. Swiftly, I put the pile of envelopes beside me back into the world of the black box in the correct order. I was petrified of being found out. Turning the key and ramming the box back under the bed, I stood up with my face still burning. I raced downstairs and flung the key back into the depths of the drawer, turned on the television and repeated my name time after time, trying to make it suit me.

I knew I would have to re-enter the world of the black box another evening to look through that precious envelope but sitting alone on the front room floor and staring at the wall would do for now with thoughts racing around my head, as I shouted, 'I am Pauline Catterson. I am Pauline Catterson.' It did not matter how many times I shouted my name. I could not make it fit.

That night in bed, I made a vow to leave the box alone for a while because the shocking evidence presented to me in that old cream envelope was enough to cope with for now. In the darkness of my room, I hurled another course of bricks onto *The Wall Against Mum* – angered by the fact she had kept my identity secret from me all my life. I was beginning to despise her, but I could not escape.

The following day at school, I hardly said a word. I refrained from sharing my secret with anyone apart from 'Dad's cloud'. For fifteen years Mum had instilled in me that I was worthless so I assumed that no one would be interested anyway. I was not important.

During the next few months, I broke out into a cold sweat each time I heard Mum go into her room. I imagined the black box finding its voice and revealing my deceitful mission to her. Each evening when I was alone, I raced through to check if the box was in the same position under her bed, confirming that it had not been investigated. Almost three years passed before I found the courage to undertake my next mission and look through the rest of the papers in that precious envelope.

('Landslide' – Fleetwood Mac – 1975)

('Nobody's Home' – Avril Lavigne – 2004)

15

Oħ No, Not Me ...

At sixteen and a half, I found a reason to stop smoking and drinking for a while. The well-tested method of remaining upright for a 'standy-uppy' or whilst 'doing it' had been unsuccessful.

I was pregnant, up the stick, had a bun in the oven. Any term you care to choose did not change the fact I was done for, and my life would be hell when Mum found out.

No pregnancy test was required. After missing my period, my body felt different. I *felt* pregnant and knew I was right. I kept it from Bert, outwardly acting as if nothing had changed, but inside I was overwhelmed, confused and totally alone. Each time I saw him, I held the truth in, and we parted with me taking my secret home alone, praying it would all go away. If I kept it to myself, then maybe my pregnancy would vanish like a puff of smoke, and we could get on with our lives. Keeping it a secret made it all less real and these irrational thoughts overtook me day after day. I knew I had to tell him sometime, but how? We were too young and immature to understand the implications of our love for each other, and the consequences had landed upon us like a ton of bricks.

What will he do when I tell him? Will he walk away like my real Mum did? Will he marry me?

Suddenly another thought cropped up. *Should I try and get rid of it myself?*

Google was not around to help in those days, and in utter desperation I tried something I had heard of at school. One evening, alone again at home, I took some of Mum's Christmas gin from the drinks cupboard and ran a steaming hot bath. Ignoring the water scalding my skin, I lay down in it, bottle in hand. I lay there motionless, with the windows misting over and my body reddening. I was petrified and consumed with guilt for what I was about to try and do. Maybe I was not pregnant at all but, if I was, how could I end the life of a baby growing inside me?

So many thoughts ran through my head and I felt sick with fear. Being unsure how much gin was the solution to all this, I took the plunge. The first perfumed mouthful made me gag, then determination kicked in and, with my eyes tight shut, I swallowed until I could swallow no more. I lay back and pummelled my stomach as hard as I dare and waited. Within five minutes of gulping the gin I flew out of the bath, and a waterfall of vomit hit the toilet pan. I was disgusted with myself but the thought of being pregnant had overpowered me. I staggered downstairs, topped up the bottle with water and, trembling all over, put it away.

Going back up to my room, I went to bed avoiding Mum's return. I lay rigid and sad waiting to see what would happen.

The next day at school was a blur, and I knew I was still pregnant. In the weeks that followed, my body changed shape and my stomach swelled into a paunch. Bert deserved to know. I felt ashamed that I had kept it from him and yet I was terrified of losing him when he found out.

One Friday night, as he was walking me home, I blurted it out. As usual, we had been sitting with friends in the back room of the pub enveloped in a blue fog of smoke as we sang along to the music blaring from the jukebox. I had drunk much less than usual, which everyone noticed, and they teased me for being a wimp. Walking home, I had only two words to say, but it took me until we were at the last bend by 'The Comp' to get them out of my mouth. I stopped walking and pulled Bert towards me, looked deep into his eyes and uttered the words that were to change our lives for ever.

'I'm pregnant.'

Bert stiffened, went white and silently pulled me closer. I ended up being late home as we spent the next half hour trying to cuddle it all away and reluctant to talk about the future. The secret was out and nothing had changed. The following night, we talked for hours and decided to keep it from Mum for a while longer.

For twenty-four weeks, I lived a desperate lie and only Bert and I knew. It was winter. Being in the sixth form at school, our uniform rules were relaxed, so I glued my black duffle coat to my body, pretending to be cold even inside the classroom. At all times, I held in my stomach muscles until they ached.

I still played hockey once a week with Mrs Honeyman coaxing me with cries of, 'Come on Burton, down that wing.'

Little did she know what she was asking me to achieve. I am still amazed that only my friend, Pauline, knew I was having a baby, and that was because I confided in her. All the other pupils and staff were oblivious to my changing shape and even quieter attitude.

More amazing and extremely sad is the fact that Mum was oblivious too. She was dumbfounded when hearing the news that her adopted daughter was with child.

On the evening that Bert told her, I said I was going to the youth club, but in reality I had arranged to meet Bert under 'our' tree. We clung on to each other, delaying the inevitable, and then he wandered off to tell Mum. Transfixed to the spot, I waited for his return, numb yet full of fear.

When Bert found the courage to knock on our door, I can imagine Mum thought the worst straightaway and that would have been Bert asking for my hand in marriage. This alternative news must have nearly killed her.

I was a quivering mess, stood shaking under 'our' tree and waiting for his return. He came back, his face ashen and, taking hold of my hands, he said, 'You'd better go straight home. Your Mum's fuming.'

'What did she say?'

'Not much. She just stood there and told me I can't see you again … and she said it'll all be dealt with.'

'What does she mean?'

'I don't know,' he whispered.

He pulled me close and we hoped our last cuddle would make it all go away. Then I had to leave. I took one last look into those beautiful blue eyes of his, begging him for the words I knew would not come and turned to walk away. He watched me go around the corner and every few yards I looked back, dawdling to delay the threat waiting for me at home and wanting to drink in my last view of Bert.

Mum greeted me like a perfect stranger and ushered me into the lounge with a face like thunder. In a daze, I heard her say, 'It will all be dealt with and then you will get on with your life as normal. You've always been a great disappointment to me, but I never thought you would do something like this. Now get out of my sight!'

I sat there shaking as I listened, eyes firmly fixed on the floor, and I remember lying in bed that night for hours, wondering what she meant as I had been far too scared to ask. I soon found out.

Mum gave Bert and me no choice whatsoever about the events to come. The following day, she kept me off school and took me to see Mr Shepherd, an obstetrician in Stockton, to confirm my condition. My face was on fire all the way there, and I felt physically sick. After a lot of form filling signed off by Mum, a nurse pointed to a bed and told me to lie down and wait. Mum sat beside me, silent and grim. I heard footsteps coming towards us and Mr Shepherd walked in, followed by six male medical students who began gawking at my body and taking notes. I lay there focused on the ceiling as my story was shared and a hand explored the inside of me. From somewhere I found my voice and with tears rolling down my face, I spluttered, 'It only happened once.'

In an even sterner voice than Mum's, Mr Shepherd retorted, 'That's what girls like you always say.' I gritted my teeth trying to control the tears.

After being examined, Mum listened to the verdict. I was just over twenty-four weeks pregnant and nothing could be done.

What does he mean? I thought.

She stormed out through the open curtains, wagging her finger at him, and exclaimed, 'We'll see about that, Mr Shepherd.'

Mr Shepherd and the students silently left my side. Once dressed, the nurse took me to Mum, who was outside, seething.

She drove her Mini furiously all the way home and once again I was told to get out of her sight, which I accepted gladly. Until that day at the hospital, I still believed it would all go away, and if not, Bert would appear round the corner from 'The Comp' and whisk me off on his white charger and marry me. My baby changed that day and became so very real.

Sadly, no white charger appeared. Instead, I heard a few mumbled telephone conversations coming from downstairs. Soon after, Mum called me down.

'We're going to London tomorrow morning to see a doctor in Harley Street. Be ready and downstairs by eight.'

There was no further explanation, but somehow I knew that Harley Street housed the most expensive clinics in England and I knew Mum could not afford it. I sat there ashamed and confused with my head down, unable to think of the right words to apologise to her.

She turned on the television and turned to me saying, 'There's no point in you sitting down here. I can't bear to look at you.'

The train journey to London was unbearable. Once again, we sat in silence with Mum staring out of the window all the way there. I read a book without digesting a word. The buildings on Harley Street were frightening in their grandeur, and my fear escalated, with me unsure of why we were there.

'It will all be dealt with,' kept on ringing in my ears.

Surely it can't be for that? I thought as we walked into the clinic.

The doctor was a small, smiley Asian man who probably dealt with lots of girls like me in such a gigantic city. The outcome turned out to be the same as in the small town of Stockton-on-Tees, however. Mum tried to argue that 'having it' was not an option and the doctor quietly said, 'Neither is an abortion, Mrs Burton. It's too late for that.'

Leaving the clinic, Mum strode off into the distance towards Hyde Park and I did my best to keep up with her, puffing and sweating at twenty-four weeks pregnant. Sitting on the nearest bench to the entrance, we shared no cuddles or words, simply the familiar blackened banana sandwiches she had prepared for the trip. I had disgraced myself and Mum would never forgive me. The relatives had been right after all.

From that day on, I kept a diary at the back of my French vocabulary jotter and poured out my feelings from day to day as my baby continued to grow. I made a monthly tally chart, counting the days until my due date in the last week of March 1971.

Now I know you'll say keeping another diary was a dangerous thing to do, since the year before Mum had found my green suede diary under the pillow. She read it from cover to cover and learned all about the goings on of a teenager in love in the 1960s. She confronted me with it after school one day, questioned me about its contents, and then tore it to shreds in front of me in my bedroom. An entire year of memories gone in an instant – along with my trust.

That frightful incident didn't stop me from keeping another diary. It had to be. It was the only way I could cope with my situation and get through it alone.

The day after we got back from Harley Street, Mum rang Mr Watts, my headmaster, to tell him the bad news, and he suggested it would be best for all concerned that I leave school immediately. 'All concerned', I took to mean the reputation of the school, and so the following Friday was to be my last day there after six years of study.

On that final Friday, I walked out of school and only Pauline knew the reason. As I puffed my way up Yarm bank and around the last bend by 'The Comp', I wished I had somewhere else to go. I knew Mum would be waiting to confront me to see if anyone had suddenly noticed my condition on that final day at school.

I was wrong.

When I walked through the front door, she pointed towards the lounge and said she wanted to talk to me. I sat on the settee with her hovering over me while she laid down the law … and the plans.

'It's all been organised for your own good,' she said in her usual matter-of-fact voice.

'Your Uncle Fred's given me as much time off work as I need, so here's what's going to happen and it's not open to discussion.'

('We Gotta Get Out of This Place' – The Animals – 1965)

('Sunshine of Your Love' – Cream – 1967)

('The Man Who Sold the World' – David Bowie – 1971)

('In My Own Time' – Family – 1971)

16

The Plan and Enactment

Mum continued talking. I sat, head down, clutching my hands and wondering what I was about to be told.

The plan was to stay with Mum's eldest sister and her husband in Alwoodley, in the City of Leeds. This was to lessen the intense shame I had brought on the whole family. I also worked out it was to whisk me away from the prying eyes of Yarm. I could almost hear the tongues starting to wag, working out why we had disappeared so suddenly.

My studies would continue, with school posting work for my 'O' level resits, having miserably failed Maths, German and History because I had been utterly busy, being in love. My resits would take place in the dining room at Auntie Dorothy's and Mum would invigilate.

Nothing new there then, I thought.

Three weeks before the birth of my baby, I was to move into an unmarried mothers' home on the other side of Leeds. *What's an unmarried mothers' home?* I wondered. I was not brave enough to ask.

'There'll be plenty of girls like you in there,' she added.

What sort of girl was I? I was not a bad girl. I was just a sad girl. A sad girl whose treasured dad had died and who had found happiness and love again with Bert. Happiness and love were the two things I had been crying out for since Dad's death, but Mum had never tried her hand at giving either.

The Leeds plan continued …

Once I was in the unmarried mothers' home, Mum would go back to work as if nothing had happened, with her head held high. She would initially pay for my stay there, but four years down the line when I reached twenty-one, I would repay her *in full* out of the money my dad had left me in trust. My baby would be put up for adoption immediately, and I would return to school, once again, as if nothing had happened.

'That's if Mr Watts'll still let you back in afterwards, but we'll deal with that when the time comes.'

She concluded our one-sided conversation by saying that if anyone asked, 'the story' would be that Mum had been extremely ill, hence the stay in Leeds.

'Tell them nothing more,' she said. 'They don't need to know.'

Every time I raised my head to ask about 'the plan', Mum cut me short with a steely stare and hurried on to the next part. I lowered my head again, listening in hazy disbelief and fighting back the tears.

The control never ceases, I thought. It goes on and on … and on.

I could not believe I had no input or choice about what was to happen to my own baby. I had no right to ask a single question or question a single thing. The shame silenced me and once she had finished, all I asked was, 'Please can I go now?' An abrupt nod of the head answered me.

A double course of bricks was catapulted and cemented firmly together on that day, on the ever-growing *Wall Against Mum*. For the second time in two years, my heart was crumbling and breaking into tiny pieces, but this time it was my fault. My throat ached; my head felt as if it would burst, but somehow I held back the tears. As I left the front room and climbed the stairs to my bedroom, I heard the key turn in the front door. Swinging round, I saw her pocket the key. She spotted me on the stairs and said once again, 'It's for your own good, Anne.'

Shaking all over, I quietly closed my bedroom door before silently screaming. Sitting down on the bed, my first thoughts were of Bert.

He needs to know … he needs to know.

With a million questions flying through my head, I lay down on my bed until I heard Mum shouting up the stairs, 'Dinner's ready.'

The atmosphere during dinner could *not* have been cut with a knife. The tension was far too thick even for that. The silence crushed me as it was surely meant to, and I cannot put into words the relief I felt when all the tidying up was finished, and I could escape upstairs once more. For the rest of the evening, I quietly played some LPs that Bert and I loved on my dear dad's record player, trying to mould a plan of my own into being, and muttering the words 'he needs to know' over and over again.

'Can I ring Pauline while you're at church, please?' I asked the following morning, expecting a negative answer.

'Yes, alright … ten minutes is your limit and tell her you'll see her when all this is over. Oh, and no going into the details.' *Yes, Mum, no, Mum, three bags full, Mum*, I thought.

All I said was, 'Thank you.'

I watched Mum drive off and grabbed the receiver to dial Pauline's house. Jitters ran right through me, but as soon as I got through, Mum's conditions of 'not going into the details' went out of the window. Hardly taking a breath, I blurted it all out and swore her to secrecy, convinced I could trust her not to say a word to anyone other than our three friends and, of course, Bert. I also believed that she would uphold the story of Mum's sudden illness if anyone asked.

Pauline and I hatched a plan to tell Bert what was going on. She would sign out from school the following Monday lunchtime and clamp a note under the windscreen wipers of his car outside 'The Skinyard', telling him everything down to the last detail. In her note, she would also ask him to ring her every Thursday night at seven o'clock, to check if she had heard anything from me. With the ten minutes nearly up and my voice trembling,

I thanked her for helping me. We hung up, almost in tears, knowing that it would be months before we saw each other again.

Hiding away in the solace of my bedroom, my very being buckled, and I slumped on the floor with my face in my hands, sobbing and wondering if Bert really cared. Suddenly, a jabbing pain in my stomach made me feel dizzy and light-headed. I prised off my top and watched in amazement as my stomach began to flutter. Then, for an instant, it pulsed outwards below my ribs, like a kick. I looked again. It *was* a kick. It had to be. No one had explained this would happen. No one had explained anything to me about being pregnant, but instinct alerted me the second it began. I just knew. That first kick became a special secret between my baby and me. After all, I had no one else to share it with. Not even Bert. Those marvellous and minute motions have stayed in my memory and in my heart, forever.

The following weekend, and four days after spending my seventeenth birthday alone, Mum and I set off for the sixty-mile journey to Leeds. Another journey fraught with silence, and I stared out of the window all the way there petrified of what was to come.

I knew Auntie Dorothy and Uncle Sam so well, as during every summer holiday in my younger years, I had stayed with them for a week. My dad and Uncle Sam had been like brothers. Both had friendly eyes that twinkled and smiled, and the two of them were full of jokes and mischief. Both of them tried to develop that same sense of humour in their respective wives, but both had failed. Uncle Sam was the closest thing to my dad I had left, and I wondered if he would still welcome me when I got there or if the 'two-headed-adopted-variety of a girl' had gone too far this time.

The semi-detached behind the streetlight - 539 King Lane,
Leeds - with the green and the 'lonely' box room.

As a child, I spent hours on the long, daisy-filled green at the front of their house searching for four-leaf clovers. Armed with my Christmas cracker magnifying glass, I became Miss Sherlock Burton with a keen eye for spotting the target. They grow in clumps, you know, and once you find one, focus on nearby ground and I almost guarantee that there will be more. Mark the words of a true and experienced four-leaf clover detective. My detective work also gave me a chance to get away from the grown-ups in the front room overlooking the green, into a safe and happy world of my own.

Now everyone knows that finding a four-leaf clover is supposed to bring you luck, and so over the years, I placed each one of the sixteen I found there on that special green, into a growing collection of Swan Vestas matchboxes, to preserve them for eternity.

It was also to make sure my life would be sixteen times luckier than the non-Sherlocks of this world. I can remember watching and waiting for either my dad or Uncle Sam to light the last match from their box, strike up their pipe, and then I would be there kneeling in front of them, asking, 'Please can I have the box for my four-leaf clovers?' Memories of happy and innocent times of the past.

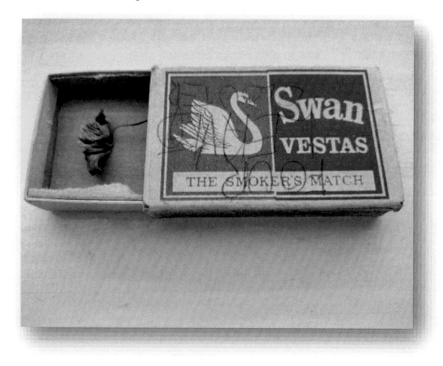

My 60-year-old four-leaf clover.

As I sat like a cramped, lifeless dummy in Mum's Mini on our way to Leeds, my faith in four-leaf clovers vanished forever.

When I walked into 539 King Lane, I was met with a scornful look, a set mouth and even colder eyes than Mum's, if that was possible. Uncle Sam held back from giving me a cuddle, but his eyes smiled at me just like in the good old days of Dad. He directed me to the box room upstairs, where I had always slept on my visits. Unpacking my things, I could hear muffled voices downstairs, and I was certain they were discussing how to move forward with me.

Now, I know it was kind of them to take us in, but somewhere along the line a little bit of love is needed. During my whole time there, it was only when Uncle Sam came home from work that I received any sort of meaningful conversation or affection, and I saw how Mum and Auntie Dorothy reacted to the kindness he offered me. 'The Look' said it all. *'That's enough ... Leave her alone ... She deserves nothing ...'*

In the coming days and weeks, the two sisters delighted in working together to offer me one thing: complete withdrawal of love, and they were masters of it. I ached for Bert to hold me and reassure me I could get through this, but he was only there in my dreams.

Each night in the box room, I scribbled my feelings and fears into my jotter. I added a strike to my tally, thankful that I had made it through another day. Then the hot tears dripped endlessly across my cheeks as I sobbed myself to sleep.

After a couple of days, Mum and I took the bus into Leeds to visit Schofield's, a high-class department store where Uncle Sam worked as manager of the men's department. I assumed we were on our way to see him, but upon me asking for confirmation, Mum raised her eyebrows and glanced at my stomach then carried on walking in front of me. We followed the signs for the fabric department and Mum told me to choose two lots of material so I could sew my own maternity smocks. In those days, patterns came in single sizes and she insisted I needed measuring before choosing the size of pattern, quietly reminding me, 'After all, you've never had a normal body. Think of all the patterns I've had to alter over the years. I'm not wasting money on the wrong pattern, Anne. Take your coat off and stand there until I find someone to measure you, and then you can go and choose your material.'

Standing there in full view of everyone, I hung my head down once again and waited, wishing the ground would swallow me up. A well-dressed assistant came over with Mum to where I was standing. When I lowered the coat I was clutching, her jaw dropped momentarily but a false smile soon shone through and I wondered if staff training included 'How to Feign False Smiles in Awkward Situations'. The assistant leaned towards Mum and lowered her voice, saying, 'Your daughter doesn't need measuring, Madam. I assume you'll be looking for a smock pattern? They already take into account her …' and she cleared her throat, ' … somewhat enlarged shape.'

For once, Mum did not feel the need to prove herself right and nodded, thanking her. My two choices of material were a warm paisley cord in two different colours. A dull green and a dull brown. Both extremely dull, as that was how I was feeling. Dull, fat and frightened. Mum let her guard down after she paid, and we ended our outing in Schofield's café. I was treated to a 'light lunch' and a long look out of the windowed wall in front of us. It was the only place to look to avoid eye contact with Mum, who must have been devastated to be seen with me in public.

That's when I hatched my plan, not quite knowing how to carry it out. Right opposite Schofield's, I spotted the Central Library. What better place to get away from the two hard-faced sisters, further my resit studies and arrange for Bert to come and meet me one weekend while I was supposedly studying. I let my thoughts develop and wondered if I dare execute the plan that had been laid in front of me.

Back at Auntie Dorothy's, I sewed my maternity smocks with haste, disgusted at their size and remembering the disco dress days when Dad was ill. My body responded overnight to the extra room the smocks offered me and also to the fact that the secret of my pregnancy was now out in the open. My bump exploded and my breasts followed suit. I began to dwell once again on how my breasts had been a problem for me.

They had attracted the wrong sort of attention from being thirteen years old. Walking down Stockton High Street before the Bert and baby days, I remember a lorry driver leaning out of his cab and shouting to my friend Gwyneth and I. Grinning from ear to ear, he said, 'I'd like to see you two fall flat on your faces!' Just a joke, I know, and on that day we laughed, but the jokes carried on for years.

The boys at school never held my eyes for long when talking to me. Instead, their gaze would drift downwards towards my enormous breasts and I wanted to scream, 'Hey, I'm up here.'

By the time I was fourteen, their taunts and teasing made me give up school swimming lessons, as I was so embarrassed hearing comments like, 'Anne Burton won't sink,' or 'We'll get a good look when she does the backstroke,' and the sniggers would echo around the swimming baths. I opted for all-girl sports like hockey and tennis – and the sad thing was I had always adored swimming.

I was seen as a 'certain sort of girl' just because I had an enormous chest, as if this type of girl could choose what size they desired by pushing a button to engage growth mode and keep it running. Even my Auntie Freda, who was plump and cuddly herself, would greet me every Saturday afternoon on our visits, with the words, 'Hello Fatty.' And I was not fat at all. I just had enormous breasts.

My Mum never protected me and laughed the remark away. Outwardly, I took it all on the chin but, inside me, those days have affected my entire life and made me hide my body from view, even in the most intimate of circumstances. All my friends' breasts stopped growing within a couple of years and their bodies grew around them in proportion, but mine continued to flourish, turning into stretched jugs. I hated them, hated the attention they caused, and made a vow to myself that one day I would get them reduced, after all this was over. For now, they were filling up like giant balloons with the impending birth of my baby.

A strict regime soon emerged at 539 King Lane. After breakfast, I escaped into the dining room, to spend my days studying for my resits with the door firmly closed on me, hiding me from view. Each day, the two sisters came to sit with me at 'coffee time' and interrogate me about my revision sessions. Little did they know that some of my time was spent surreptitiously scribbling lyrics from songs playing on the radio in the background. Songs relevant to Bert, the baby and I, and songs that bring a lump to my throat when I hear them on the radio, even now. They take me straight back to those dark days in Leeds. The most special song during those dreadful days was 'Your Song' by Elton John, which I silently told my unborn baby was for her. It was *her* song.

I was so young. I was so frightened and alone, even though I was surrounded by familiar people, and I knew as I sobbed myself to sleep each night that the next day would be worse. My baby communicated with me by frequently kicking and turning over letting me know she was fine, and that one day soon, we would meet. Some nights I told my baby I would never let her go. We would manage somehow, and I would give her all the love I had lacked before her dad came along. Other nights I whispered gently to her through the darkness saying her dad would come and rescue us and we would struggle through life together as a little family, full of love and hope. I secretly wrote my jotter diary each night as a record of the 'Countdown to Baby' days, and one day I promised myself I would give it to her along with a copy of 'Your Song'.

The highlight of each week was a phone call from my friends back home keeping me up to date with what was happening in their lives. The phone was in the hall so for a few minutes I had relative privacy. One particular friend was determined that Bert was cheating on me and named the girl involved. Other friends just wanted to tell me their news and ask how I was managing. Pauline and I chattered on about all sorts and then she would write down a whispered message for Bert and pass it on to him. I told her when I would be at the phone box outside the local shops in Alwoodley each week, so he could ring me from the phone box in Yarm, and we could pretend to be together for a few minutes on his lunch break. It was our lifeline. I chose to ignore the particular friend's gossip and kept on believing that Bert loved me and only me and would always be faithful. After all, I was carrying his baby.

I often waddled down to those shops in my break from revision at lunchtimes. It was a means of escaping from the house and it also meant that 'phone call day' did not arouse suspicion. Each week, when Bert rang me, those calls flew by and were mostly spent arranging a time to meet in the Central Library the following Saturday.

Yes, I had dared to execute my plan. Permission to go to the library each Saturday was unsmilingly sanctioned one evening when Uncle Sam was around, as I knew he would reason with Mum if she refused.

Our arrangement to meet was always a tentative one, as so much could go wrong before the day. Bert's car might break down or he may have to work, but usually the plan worked and it was heaven to see him. Whispering away in the library, we sat as close as we dare, dreaming of life back home in the months to come. Each time he came, I prayed that he would propose to me there and then so that we could keep our baby. Towards the end of each meeting, the sadness descended knowing it was not to be. Wandering outside hand in hand, we found the strength to say goodbye with a promise from him he would return the following week.

Trying to ignore the despair, I traipsed back to the bus station with faith in my heart that Bert was mine, and he was returning to Yarm knowing that his baby had heard her dad's voice once more. We both understood on those occasions it could be for the last time.

In my last week at Auntie Dorothy's, the particular friend, Sue, whose gossip I chose to ignore, rang to announce she had spotted Bert walking down the High Street with the same girl again. The following Saturday was to be my last meeting with him before moving into Falloden Nursing Home. On the way to the library that day, what Sue had said built up in my mind, and I decided to tackle him. Sitting on the bus with dark clouds gathering outside, I practised my speech, knowing full well the words might not materialise when I saw him if my courage evaporated. All the best laid plans, as they say. After an hour in the library, my heart sank as the realisation set in. Bert was not coming.

I tried to believe he would still turn up, and sat there pretending to revise, surrounded by students and watching the entrance, hoping he would walk in. At last, with a heaviness descending, I collected my school books together and left the building with my heart breaking.

How much worse can my life become? I thought. I trusted Bert and he had let me down. From that day on, I never put my full trust in anyone because I knew the sorrow would be too much to bear if it was anything like I felt that day in Leeds.

I was in a daze all the way back, staring through the raindrops lashing against the window of the bus and thinking of him, knowing that I would be going into Falloden the following week. That Saturday had been our last chance to hold each other and for our baby to hear his voice.

('Your Song' – Elton John – 1971)

('Stand By Me' – Ben E King – 1961)

('I Heard it Through the Grapevine' – Marvin Gaye – 1968)

('Under the Bridge' – Red Hot Chilli Peppers – 1992)

17

The Place from Hell

In early March 1971, plans were set in place to move me into Falloden Nursing Home for three weeks before the expected birth of my baby.

That is easy, you may think. *You pays your money and you moves yourself in.*

No ... no ... no. That's not the way to do it.

'You have to pass an interview to show yourself as suitable first.' Well, that is what Mum told me, moments before we set off to go there.

What does she mean? I asked myself. *This is an unmarried mothers' place, isn't it? I am pregnant and unmarried so I must be suitable*, I thought. *Why do I need an interview?*

I did not ask for any answers. As usual, there was no point.

She and I made our way in her trusty orange Mini to Falloden Nursing Home in Chapel Allerton, on the other side of Leeds. It was becoming almost impossible for me to manoeuvre my way in and out of her tiny car as my body continued to explode and my movements were increasingly limited. I was huge. I was also petrified and despised her for what she was about to make me do.

My first sight of Falloden sent wave after wave of shivers through me, until a protective numbness took me over as I had no choice but to accept whatever was going to be thrown my way. I was determined to get through it all. I was consciously trying to keep my emotions in check, becoming numb and trying not to let the sadness overwhelm me.

Falloden Nursing Home was set in extensive leafy grounds just like

Cleveland, my primary school had been all those years ago, but this place emitted such a hostile feeling from the outset. We drove in silence through the narrow entrance flanked by two tall stone pillars, after which the light of the day disappeared, engulfing us in overhanging foliage, and it was like entering a deep, dark tunnel from which there was no escape. Hurtling towards hell. I had to focus on believing there would be a light at the end of that tunnel one day. I was suffocating in the darkness even though it was broad daylight.

Knocking firmly on the front door, Mum turned to me exuding that familiar coldness, 'This is it then, Anne, and it's all your own fault.' I did not have the inclination or the time to reply.

The door opened and a tall, stern-faced member of staff, dressed in white, nodded at us and let us into a large, square hallway. It was like stepping back in time to Victorian days. Huge, high ceilings like our house in Yarm and dark-coloured wallpaper surrounded us. She told us to sit down, saying, 'Wait here please,' and off she went along a corridor with a final narrow-eyed glance back at us. The minutes ticked by and I wanted to run. To run away from this place and keep right on running, back to a time of innocence when Dad was alive, and I was loved completely. Of course, that would have been impossible. My back ached continuously and my bladder leaked with the slightest movement. And Dad was dead. Another suffocating silence ensued and I disappeared into the world of my own thoughts again.

Mrs Lodge, a small, dark-haired lady and the matron of Falloden, bustled towards us and invited us into her salubrious-looking office. Although I was terrified, she put me at ease. She had a soft voice and smiling eyes, something I was not used to of late. We were served tea and biscuits and told that Dr Bloomfield would be joining us soon. He was the doctor who had examined me once a week during my stay at Auntie Dorothy's, to check that all was going according to plan. And the next stage of the plan was to be started right there, right then.

As soon as he joined us, the meeting began. Mrs Lodge asked Dr Bloomfield if there were any problems with my health or the pregnancy itself – to which he replied there were none. She then asked me to confirm that the health of the baby's father was good and questioned me further, asking if he had ever encountered health problems – to which I replied he had not. The word 'health' made me suspicious and reality erupted in my head as I realised why she was asking. She then explained, in a very matter-of-fact way, that I would be required to sign some forms.

'Your signature means that your baby can be adopted and you can't change your mind after the birth.' She paused for a moment and then asked me if I understood. I stared at her in a daze and unable to speak.

What happened to the interview? I thought. *When does that start? That must come before any form signing?*

I switched my gaze to Mum, trying to reach into her soul, and silently begged her with my whole being to take me away from this place and let me keep my baby. All was quiet, all was still and the room slowly started to spin as I felt the blood draining from my face. No one in the room knew what to say so Mrs Lodge turned her attention to Mum and asked how she would be paying for my stay. *How clinical,* I thought.

This stirred Mum into action as she explained without any trace of emotion, 'I'll be paying by cheque and Anne will repay me in full on her twenty-first birthday with the money her dad put into a trust fund for her.' Mrs Lodge only had a moment to respond by raising her eyebrows as Mum carried on and told her, 'We're ready to sign the forms now.'

I sat there, dumbfounded, listening to Mum reinforcing her coldness and cruelty.

How dare you keep on taking control of my life. What about me and my baby? These thoughts shot through my head within seconds and another enormous, everlasting, never-to-be-forgotten shedload of bricks flew into place on *The Wall Against Mum.*

She had not even had the guts to tell me the truth before we set off that day. 'An interview', she had said. Just an interview. Now here I was being forced to sign my baby's life away.

In amongst all the hatred I felt for her, realisation set in. I had to abide by her decision. When all this was over, I would be going back to another sort of prison. I had nowhere else to go. That did not seem like a light at the end of this deep, dark Falloden tunnel, merely a continuation of being pulled down by her pointing out how imperfect I was while controlling my every move. I had no hope left.

Anyway who was this 'we' Mum spoke about? It must be me who needed to sign the forms, and once I had signed them my baby would not be mine any more. I would never be able to hold her and look at her, smell her special baby smell, comfort and protect her and guide her through life. Someone else would be doing all that.

Glancing at Mum with her gloved hands clutching the handbag sat staunchly on her knee and her mouth set in a thin hard line, I tried to reach into her soul once more. I looked deep into her eyes begging for a reprieve, but I found nothing there. Absolutely nothing.

'Mum … *please* … don't make me do this,' I begged out loud, but she sat there bolt upright, looking straight ahead and avoiding my plea.

Everything seemed to go into slow motion as form after form was put in front of me. Each time before signing, I glanced at Mum still silently begging her, but it was too late. The deed had been done. After a brief goodbye, Mum and I left Mrs Lodge's office. Needless to say, we drove back to Alwoodley in silence. The ability to trust anyone at all had been snatched away from me for the second time in a week.

Two days later, we drove back into the tunnel of despair at Falloden. Mum disposed of me in the hallway along with my small blue suitcase, and a nurse escorted me up a wonderfully wide staircase, carpeted with plush red pile carpet and the same dark wallpaper as before adorning the walls. Reaching the landing, I was guided along a narrow corridor and immediately noticed that the surroundings were becoming less grand.

Round another corner and I was ushered into a room in the unmarried mothers' quarters of the home, to see three other girls sitting quietly in hospital-type armchairs, with their heads lowered. As we entered, they looked up at me and a momentary smile lit up their faces. The nurse pointed to my bed and a wardrobe in one corner and told me to unpack. Then she left and shut the door behind her without a word. That was the only time I saw that wonderful staircase until the day of my departure. I soon learned that 'girls like us' were expected to use what had in the past been the servants' stairs at the back of the house.

The three girls shyly introduced themselves. Karen, Jennifer and Avril. Quiet, sad, lonely girls, just like me. All three of them had been in long-term relationships before being hidden away in Falloden, far away from their individual hometowns of Wakefield, Bradford and York. In a way that made me feel better, knowing that Mum was not the only mum in the world ashamed of her daughter. There were other mums around as cruel and face-saving as mine. At least I felt less alone in the world knowing that.

Our room was spotlessly clean, with a view to the outside world that we all craved. Four metal hospital beds with sweaty waterproof mattress covers and starched white sheets were our place of rest. We were allowed basic personal belongings such as soap, shampoo, toothbrushes and toothpaste, as long as they were kept neatly in a wash bag in the drawer of our bedside table. When they saw me unpacking my radio, the other girls told me that luxuries like that were expressly forbidden and to hide it before it got confiscated. Another lifeline gone for me, considering how much I adored music, and I know it could have helped me through.

Karen and Avril were my age and Jennifer was the grown-up one at eighteen years old. We had all lived through the '60s and loved pop music, so we used to sing together quietly in our room when we were finished with our chores. Singing brought us together, and we shared personal memories attached to each song we sang. Some memories made us laugh and others made us sob, but the singing helped us to bond and get through those dreadful days waiting for our babies to be born and taken away forever. We would sing with our eyes firmly fixed on the doorknob of our room which, when it turned, signalled a member of staff about to enter and time for the singing to stop. Singing was forbidden and we all knew that.

On my first afternoon at Falloden, a nurse took me down the servants' staircase to meet Sister Mac. She was small and slight with a deep, embedded frown and pale smoker's lips. I have never met anyone like her since my days at Falloden, and I am eternally grateful for that. She was dressed as most nursing sisters were back then: more starch about her dark blue uniform than a whole sack of potatoes. Her white hat was tall with a navy rim and placed immaculately on her head like a crown. Protruding from under it was heavily sprayed, greying brown hair. The face underneath the hairdo was unyielding and bitter and her voice was like that of a Yorkshire Cruella de Vil. She sat me down in her office and looked right through me with total disdain. Her broad, booming dialect belied her stature as it travelled across the room towards me.

'Well, little Miss Clever Clogs … before I tell you the rules, I want you to think of the shame you've brought on your family …' and she paused giving me time to feel worse than I already did. 'I know you're scared and worried, but that's what happens to girls like you. No respect for your elders, that's what I say. It's time to toe the line now, do the best for your baby by giving it to someone who can look after it properly and *woe betide you* if you disobey any of the rules. Do you understand what I'm saying?'

Just as had happened in Mrs Lodge's office, I could not reply. The words would not come. Instead, I nodded and, by the look she gave me, I knew I had been seen as impertinent for not answering properly.

She read out the rules and routines of Falloden Nursing Home, unmarried mothers' section and abortion section only, and I had to sign to confirm I understood and would abide by them. Here we go then – and there were many …

No radios.

No singing.

No loud voices.

No magazines or newspapers.

No phone calls.

Permitted visitors only.

No food to be brought in by visitors (apart from fruit).

No letters from friends unless agreed by parent(s) of the unmarried mother.

Sister Mac continued, 'You'll be woken up at six and be expected in the kitchen by half past, ready for your daily chores. Use the back stairs at all times and *do not* go near the front stairs. They're for normal people, not girls like you.'

Who were the normal people? I wondered, but soon worked out that she must mean the married mothers, the staff and the couples coming to take our babies away.

'At eight o'clock you'll have breakfast in the unmarried mothers' dining room and then straight back to the kitchen until lunchtime: one o'clock sharp. After lunch, you'll have a half-hour break before you finish your chores for the day. You're expected to be in bed by nine thirty, with lights out and complete silence by ten o'clock.'

What other kind of silence is there? I thought.

She spouted all this out with her head held high, looking down her nose at me as if I was a piece of trash – which I was beginning to believe I probably was.

'You can go now and don't forget to report to the kitchen by half past six tomorrow morning.' That said, she carried on with her paperwork, leaving me to wonder whether to say 'thank you', having been taught to do so all my life.

'Thank you, Sister Mac,' I muttered, and scurried off feeling just like the piece of trash she had looked at down her nose.

Most of the staff were of the same ilk as Sister Mac, apart from Mrs Lodge and two others. One was the cook-cum-general-kitchenhand who was called Beryl. She was tall and scrawny with short, highlighted hair, and completely down to earth. The other was Anna, my favourite nurse from the outset. She had a sense of humour and made the four of us feel like human beings again. She was kind and understanding with a soft Irish lilt, twinkling blue eyes and thick dark hair, severely scraped back into a bun, all topped off by her nurse's hat. We avoided contact with the rest of the staff whenever possible as the critical looks they gave us were too much to bear.

On my first full day, Mrs Lodge took me into the kitchen to meet Beryl. As she left she added some rules of her own, 'You must not talk to any of the other girls until all your chores are completed. If you disobey there will be a punishment,' which did not even bear thinking about.

'Part of your duties will be to set the tables in the married mothers' dining room. Any communication with them is totally forbidden. I'm sure you understand why.'

The following morning Beryl greeted me with a fleeting smile and showed me around the kitchen, explaining how to set about my chores. Some were much more achievable than others in my thirty-sixth week of pregnancy. It was torture trying to complete the heavy physical tasks and we all believed that the point was to make us suffer and fill us with shame and remorse, directing us to the conclusion that if we had been good girls, we would not have had to endure any of it. Those feelings consumed us every day, but I tried to keep my chin up as best I could and tell myself that keeping busy would make the time in Falloden go more quickly. Often, that was almost impossible to do. There were days when I wanted to give up completely and crawl into a corner and die, and I found that crying did not ease the suffering at all.

In that abysmal place, I was fortunate, I suppose, to spend most of my days with Beryl. She had a kind heart and a genuine smile even if she hardly dare show it. Still, my chores seemed endless.

I had five chores expected of me during my stay, one of which was to clean the three industrial cookers until they shone inside and out. Slowly squatting down, I balanced my huge belly while I transferred all my weight onto my hands, lowering my knees to the floor at the same time. Reaching into the back of the ovens squashed my enormous bump which in turn squashed my bladder, and being excused for toilet breaks was extremely frequent. Thank goodness Beryl understood and let me go. Kneeling caused my legs to cramp and the pain that shot through them was almost unbearable. It went on until, holding onto one of the cookers, I managed to hoist myself and my baby back up to a standing position to rub and shake my legs, knowing that I had to finish the task and go through the cramps all over again.

Each day, I was made to scrub the tiled floor throughout the enormous kitchen. Back down on my knees, I manoeuvred and dragged the steel bucket full of hot water across the floor and scrubbed and dried, scrubbed and dried until it gleamed once more. I planned my route for each part of the floor to end up at one of the cookers, so I had something to heave myself back up on, before waddling to the sink to change or empty the water.

Another chore was to load a huge wooden trolley with all the tableware needed for the three meals a day in every one of the three dining rooms. I was terrified I would break something and my neck was like a rod until I had completed the task. As soon as the married mothers', the unmarried mothers and the girls staying in overnight for an abortion had left their respective dining rooms, I had it all to load up again and cart back to the kitchen ready to wash up.

Looking on the bright side, this task gave me the chance to see the married mothers' dining room. How different it was from ours and the dining room of the girls there for an abortion. Decorated with sumptuous wallpaper, each table was set with a starched and ironed tablecloth, damask napkins, water jugs and tumblers. I had to ensure that all the cutlery was spotless and in the right place for the different courses provided. Everything had to be shipshape. Our dining room had painted walls, hard wooden chairs, bare Formica tables and 'girls like us' did not have the luxury of water with their meals. Setting the tables was the closest thing to enjoyment in my time at Falloden, even though I was scared of mucking it up and breaking something. It was a solitary job and gave me time for my own thoughts about Bert and my baby, who day by day was getting bigger and closer to being born.

The questions circled round in my head and I prayed for an angel to come to me at night and answer them. *Will I see the couple who are coming to take my baby away? Will I ever know where she's gone? Will they be kind to her and give her love?*

I knew in my heart that it did not matter whether I got to see them and it might be even more painful if I knew where my baby had gone. As usual I would have no say. I had signed the forms that took all the decision making away from me.

Back in the kitchen at Falloden, I knew all of my chores must be completed exactly as demanded by 'The Place From Hell'. Nowadays, not one woman, at least in our country, should ever have to undergo such cruelty and danger while pregnant. I hope with all my heart that I am correct.

The coal scuttle chore was almost impossible. I was thirty-six weeks pregnant and at five foot nothing I was barely strong enough to complete it, but somehow and from somewhere, I found the strength. Something kept me going and 'Dad's cloud' came into play once more as I performed this chore. Three times a day I made my way over the moss-covered yard to the huge coal sheds behind the kitchen. After filling ten tall coal scuttles right up to the brim, I carried them back, two at a time, contorted with pain. They wrenched every muscle in my body and my stomach in particular. I was petrified of damaging my baby, but I had no choice. I felt like a slave from the past and not a seventeen-year-old girl whose stay in this horrendous home had been so handsomely paid for. I had never been afraid of physical work but to put my unborn baby at risk was so utterly cruel and wrong. Cruel and wrong of Falloden and cruel and wrong of Mum. *'It's all your own fault,'* kept on ringing in my ears.

The ethos of Falloden was one of pure punishment, and the cruelty that ran alongside it would ensure that 'girls like us' thought long and hard on our return to normal life before allowing another member of the male species to approach us with similar intent. The staff were aware that our memories would never fade, and our hurt would lie deep within us for eternity. We would remember every moment in that dreadful place. Our throats would ache, our eyes would brim over and our hearts would carry on breaking for years afterwards with each of those memories. And they were right. Even though Falloden Nursing Home burned down to the ground in the '80s, the memories are as vivid today as they were back then when Karen, Avril, Jennifer and I shared a room.

I completed the worst chore of all six times only. Thank goodness for small mercies. Twice a week, Beryl pointed to the high, square-topped wooden stool and told me to clean the windows which spanned one whole wall of the kitchen. After filling the enormous steel bucket with cold water and white vinegar, I rubbed the solution all over the windows and then dried them off. Using old newspapers, I polished them until – like the floor – they gleamed. And I performed this terrible trick on a high wooden stool, the height of a bar stool today.

Nicknaming it the three-step challenge, I hauled myself up onto my knees before standing up by steadying myself and hanging onto a window frame catch, leaning forward to try and keep my balance and stop the stool from toppling over. My heart hammered throughout. Forbidden protection was offered as Beryl hovered close by, listening for other staff approaching, and the relief on our faces when I had finished turned into a smile and the beginning of a bond between us. She praised me for a job well done and the fear of falling passed for another few days.

Every day after finishing my chores, my clothes were spattered with grease or dirt and I had noticed the twin-tub washing machines in a room behind the kitchen. Investigating further, I spotted a notice that shone out loud and clear: *For Falloden use only*. The 'girls like us' were relegated to washing by hand, although we were allowed to use the washing lines in the mossy yard. All our big knickers hung outside on show to all who cared to look as they passed by in the street beyond. And in my case, bras that resembled parachutes swung and danced there too. White parachutes of course. One thing my stay at Falloden taught me was to consolidate the fact that hard work is necessary and never did anyone any harm. Apart from, of course, if the window-washing stool had toppled and then you may not be reading this, and my baby may not have survived.

Each evening, after our chores were done for the day, my three inmates and I sat in the confines of our room, aching and exhausted. This was our free time. We compared how our pregnant bodies had coped with the day, trying to work out how to mend anything that hurt without having a clue what to do. We were trying to look out for each other in the best way we could.

We quietly chatted about our fears of what would happen when the time came. We got to know about each other's lives, listening to snippets of news received by letter from our families. We comforted each other when we burst into tears and became so close for the duration of our stay, although none of us ever built a friendship that lasted after those torturous Falloden days. Our lives had been turned upside down by the very fact that we were all there for the same reason, and we held back from giving ourselves completely to one another. We knew we should not have been there. It was wrong, and we went through each day with one emotion at the forefront of our minds: shame, followed closely by remorse and fear.

There was momentary excitement when we received letters from permitted friends telling us what was happening in our hometowns. The gossip, the break-up of relationships, people we knew who had started going out together, and our friends asking if we had heard the new record by so-and-so – which of course we had not, as music was forbidden. All the letters that came for me were from Pauline, they were full of news and helped me to hold on to my sanity. Sometimes another secret letter was hidden inside Pauline's letter. Oh, what joy! To receive a letter from my best friend was so comforting and if it also contained another letter, a love letter from Bert, it kept me happy for days. The content of Bert's letters was not shared with any of my roommates. Those letters were for my eyes only. I used to fold each one and place it in a white paper bag and push the bag into the toes of my purple, suede platform boots, brought into Falloden with me for the day of my release. The letters were carefully hidden and re-read again and again in the toilets.

Bert's letters helped me to dismiss the unkind thoughts I had of him when I was at the end of my tether, and I tried to believe he would be there, waiting for me, when I eventually returned home without our baby.

Sadly settling down at night in a room with three other girls, sleep did not come easy and my mind often began to whirr. *How could Mum adopt me and then make me give up my own baby for adoption?*

It was like a vicious circle spinning round and round. I imagined the feelings my real mum had felt when she was carrying me, and now I was carrying my own baby, and her precious granddaughter. Both of us in the same situation at different times. Both of us knowing that our babies were to be taken away. I wondered if she had been as sad as I was, or if all those years ago, she made a conscious and calculated decision to get rid of me.

My bedtime thoughts came to an abrupt end one night when Avril went into labour in the bed right opposite me. She tossed about, putting up with the pain for hours, and begged us not to call anyone. None of us knew what to do, none of us had heard sounds remotely like that before. Karen, Jennifer and I were convinced she was dying or that some harm would come to her and her baby, with the excruciating sounds of pain pouring out of her. It was petrifying for all of us. She was in real labour and going to have a real baby very soon, and we had to be strong for her. The three of us sat up in bed, watching over her and listening to the pain that must be so horrific for sounds like that to come from a human being. We also knew in the back of our minds that our time would come soon, and hearing those dreadful noises made it worse for all of us. It turned our pregnancies into a shocking reality. The three of us were shaking as we gathered around her bed, holding her hands in turn, to try and console her.

Suddenly a member of staff came flying in, having heard the incredible wails and screams. She wheeled Avril out and we were left wondering where she had gone.

Jennifer took charge saying, 'She'll have gone to the delivery room.'

We did not know what a delivery room was, and we had no idea where it was, having never been shown it. Hours and hours passed and eventually Avril was wheeled back into our room looking drained and as white as a sheet. She returned alone without her baby. Her eyes were dazed and blank and, after what seemed like hours, she fell asleep.

The days dragged by with Karen, Jennifer and I completing our daily chores with increased slowness and all finding it virtually impossible to lift and carry anything heavy around.

Avril's routine changed completely. She was confined to bed for a few days and because her breasts were full of milk, she was expected to breastfeed a baby. Not her own baby of course. That would never do.

The baby boy that Avril had given birth to had been taken away immediately and Avril had never seen him at all. She would have to live for the rest of her life without being able to picture his tiny newborn face. At feeding times, she sat in bed, propped up by pillows, still with a face as white as a sheet and her eyes red and swollen. Even though we did what we could to cheer her up, it did not work at all.

There were two adjoining rooms to ours, each housing four more 'girls like us'. We were only allowed to communicate at mealtimes and no way could we visit each other's rooms. Each feeding time, a nurse would bring Avril a different baby from the unmarried mothers' nursery, complete with a wrist tag bearing the mother's name. Avril would hold it and feed it with her very own milk from her very own breasts, a baby from one of the girls in the adjoining rooms. A complete stranger's baby.

How disgusting and evil is that? we all thought.

'How can they get away with it?' we asked each other. We had no answers.

We could all see the various babies that were brought in and hear the baby suckling on the milk from Avril's breasts. The staff told us that we must never cross the room to get a closer look at the tiny bundle in her arms. We all religiously abided by that rule as we knew there would be terrible consequences if we did not. Still, we were amazed to see a newborn baby, and even though it was a dreadful thing that Avril was expected to do, we could not take our eyes off that baby with the wrist tag, not even sure whether she was feeding a boy or a girl. She avoided reading the name on the tag altogether and simply did her duty and handed the baby back to the nurse when she came to collect it.

Two days later, the unthinkable happened. It was an evening feed time and a baby was brought as usual. Avril suddenly started screaming at the top of her voice, her eyes wide with terror, and in the split second that followed we saw her fling the baby onto the bed with a cry of, 'That's my baby!' and she started sobbing her heart out. A member of staff must have heard the commotion, realised what had happened, and came dashing in, grabbed the baby and departed. And that was that. No comfort was ever offered from the nurse involved, no apology, merely a baby taken away for the second time. Avril was distraught for days after that and we could not find a way to soothe her.

'That's why I've never looked at the name tags,' she sobbed. 'Cos I knew one day, it'd be mine.'

The following feeding time, Avril was handed another baby and told to get on with it. We realised that nothing was beyond the staff in 'The Place From Hell', and we lived in fear every day wondering what might happen next.

One by one, Karen and Jennifer went into labour. They were wheeled away and came back without their babies. Each feeding time after that, three babies were brought into the room of the 'girls like us'. Suffice it to say that the rules of keeping our distance were blatantly abused from the day Avril held her own baby for the first and last time. We were all involved in checking each baby's name tag before the allotted feeder held them to their breast, to make sure it was a baby from one of the girls next door. You may think we had found a perfect solution, and it worked until the day Karen was given Jennifer's baby and all we heard as Karen looked across at her and whispered was, 'Jennifer, this is yours.'

Jennifer started to slowly shake her head ignoring what she had heard and continued to feed her allotted baby as she knew there was no option. Not once did her head come up to look across towards Karen's bed and the baby at Karen's breast. As soon as the babies had been taken back to the nursery, she began to tremble and sob. Slowly lying down without looking at any of us, she hid her face in the pillow and broke her heart.

Who are the people who run this place? I thought. *Are they robots?* Not on your life! Even robots could have been programmed to show more compassion, I am sure.

('Love the One You're With' – Crosby, Stills and Nash – 1970)

('Chirpy Chirpy Cheep Cheep' – Middle of the Road – 1971)

18

Elizabeth Nicole Burton

On the morning of Saturday April 3rd, 1971, at precisely twenty-seven minutes past ten, Elizabeth Nicole Burton flew into this world, head first as I had. The second baby had landed. My beautiful baby girl and I were together for an unforgettable but fleeting moment.

Mum had been visiting me some days on our lunchtime break, and I dreaded her arrival. She would march into our room, cast a disparaging glance at my three Falloden friends and sit staunch and upright in a chair by my bed, neither of us knowing what to say to each other. I had no news to report.

Was I going to tell her I had got a letter from Pauline containing a secret letter from Bert? Was I going to tell her that she made me feel sick whenever I saw her walk through the door? There was no point.

On each visit, her first words swelled the anger and hatred I felt for her. 'Oh, you look better today.'

How was I supposed to answer that? What did it mean? I worked out that her words lessened her guilt by announcing that I was looking better.

But the deed had been done. She had forced me to sign my baby away and there was nothing to say to the frightful woman sitting by my side. I held onto my strength with both hands and kept my silence, apart from answering direct questions with the politeness drummed into me over the years kicking in, as I answered with as few words as possible. My Falloden friends sat nearby pretending not to listen and rooting for me. We all despised our mothers, and they were grateful that their parents hardly visited, living further away.

The week before Nicole was born, Mum told me she was going back home to Yarm the following day. She needed to return to work and Auntie Dorothy and Uncle Sam would take over visiting duties. Initially, I was relieved. No more disgusting looks being flung at me on her visits yet the thought of my hard-faced auntie sitting by my bed was just as unbearable.

I suddenly realised that, although I despised Mum for forcing me to sign my baby away, being in Falloden without her close by would be even more terrifying than her visits. She was the one person who had stood by me. At the end of the day she had not disowned me, and for completely selfish reasons I wanted her to stay in Leeds to give me someone to rely on if I could not cope with it all. Part of me still clung on to the hope that when my baby was born, Mum would see her, change her mind and let me keep her. We would go home together, and I would guide my baby through life. I believed it was still possible because the other option was far too painful for me to accept.

I clambered into bed that night hearing the rustle of waterproof sheets as we all settled down, obeying the ten o'clock lights out and (complete) silence rule. Trying to get comfortable, my stomach felt strange. It was rock solid, like an over-inflated football about to burst. I lay there in the dark, wide awake with my hand on my stomach, thinking of Bert and where he might be, and hot tears poured down my cheeks.

After all, it was Friday night and in our old world of Bert and Anne, we would have been together hand in hand or wrapped around each other in Bert's big black car. The tears slowly subsided as thoughts of Bert faded into the background. Cradling my stomach, I was aware that my baby was peaceful and still unlike other nights over the last few weeks. Something was pushing my stomach downwards and crampy pains hit my back in waves which I ignored, frightened to alert anyone. They petered out and I drifted off to the land of dreams.

At quarter past five the next morning, I woke up with a start and straight away I knew that something had happened in the night that could not be ignored. My bed was absolutely soaking. Avril and Jennifer had already made sure I knew what that wet bed meant, and I was petrified. My waters had broken and it was time to call someone. I had a red button by my bed for emergencies – which I had never used. It took me ages to press it because I was trying to find the courage to lift the sheets and see what had happened to me.

Maybe there'll be a baby there? I thought. *Maybe I'm bleeding to death?* Why had no one explained what to do next? *Press ... Go on ... press it*, I told myself, but I dared not.

I held my breath and lifted the sheets. There was no blood. I looked harder and there was no baby, alive or dead. All I could see was a soaking wet puddle; I was laid in it, drowning completely, and I knew my time had come. My baby was on her way.

*Press ... Press it. M*y hand was shaking as I hit the emergency button, wondering who would come and what would happen next. Relief flooded through me as I saw Anna enter the room. She was the only kind nurse in the whole of Falloden, and as I'd got to know and trust her more, I'd almost begged for her help.

'Can you be with me when it's my turn? Please, Anna, I'm so scared.'

Quietly she explained that she worked shifts and it would depend on whether she was working at the right time. Well, now my time was here and so was Anna. I told her what had happened and she helped me out of bed, examined the sodden sheets and confirmed that my waters had indeed broken. Smiling at me she added, 'And don't worry, there's no baby under there. I'm afraid it's not as easy as that.'

Coming back with some clean bedding, I sat watching her, gripping both arms of the chair Mum had used on her visits. She came and knelt in front of me, took my hands in hers and whispered, 'Where are your pains, Anne?'

'It's only my back but it's different today. It's lower down.'

Anna suggested I get back into bed and call for her when the pains became worse. I was terrified and seized the opportunity to ask her what to expect. We sat for a while in the dim light of the room, talking in hushed tones about contractions and all words associated with giving birth. For the first time I understood most of what was about to happen, and it scared me to death, but somehow I knew my baby and I would fight through it all together.

Within the next hour, my contractions started with a vengeance but I still managed to eat some buttered toast and down a cup of tea that another less kindly looking nurse offered me. I was starving. The other girls woke up one by one and realised what was happening. It must have been terrible for them to watch me as their precious babies had already been taken away.

Anna came back in every half hour, to check I was managing with my spaced-out contractions, and at exactly eight o'clock she came in to say goodbye. I was not prepared for the fact she was going off duty, and I started sobbing uncontrollably. The contractions were so fierce and my emotions erupted. I felt embarrassed about breaking down publicly for the first time in that awful place and allowing anyone, even Anna, to see that I could not cope. She sat me up and gently pulled me towards her, 'I'll go and see if I can stay. If they let me, I won't leave your side. I promise.'

Lovely Anna, she was true to her word. She was the one who wheeled me into the delivery room and strapped up my feet in stirrups before she cleaned my private parts. She chattered away of her life back in Ireland as my contractions got longer, stronger and more frequent. The agony shot through the core of my whole body and the pain was so intense. It was surging right through me and twisting itself deep inside me and growing ever stronger until I wanted to die. It was overtaking me and I wanted to scream and wail that I could bear it no longer, but I dared not let go. This was my punishment for being bad and there was no way out. Then the pain moved up another gear making my face contort and drip with sweat. Groans and high-pitched screams exploded from me and I could not stop them. Eventually, I had to accept the gas and air that Anna had offered me earlier, saying, 'I'll be in big, big trouble if they see me giving you this. You girls are not allowed it.'

And so I had refused the first time around because there was no way I wanted to get her into trouble, but now the pain was becoming too much to bear.

Holding the rubber mask in place, everything was somewhat blurred until I heard Anna's voice saying, 'Push, Anne. Push.'

I did my best, listening from afar after the gas and air had kicked in. My body felt as if it was splitting in two and the effort needed to obey Anna's instructions was impossible to find.

Fight ... go on, fight, I told myself as I heard Anna somewhere in the distance shouting, 'Push, Anne. Come on girl, you can do it. One more push.'

Believing I was dying, I pushed for the last time and my baby entered the world. 'It's a girl,' Anna confirmed, but I already knew that.

Elizabeth Nicole Burton and I met for the first time as she shot upwards and came flying towards me out of my body, facing forwards, as if we could not wait to get a glimpse of each other. She opened her eyes and we drank each other in for what seemed like an age. It could only have been a few seconds but that first picture remains in my memory. Maybe it was Anna who held her up so that we could meet? I will never know. Elizabeth Nicole then opened her lungs to show me what strength they had as she cried and cried. Then Anna took her away.

A nameless nurse came in and fourteen stitches later, after she had gone, Anna returned. She laid Nicole in my arms and stood back, smiling. I will never know if that was allowed either. I only know it had not happened to Avril, Karen or Jennifer, but there I was holding my baby. I really was. My very own baby. My own baby girl.

As I drank in her newborn features, Anna said, 'Two minutes,' and I nodded without a word.

My baby was the most beautiful person I had ever seen. She had a face that cried out for me to keep her, so pink and new with gorgeous blue eyes and a mop of jet-black hair. She had a cleft in her chin just like me. She had ten, tiny spade-shaped fingernails just like mine. Her body was tiny but I held her as tight as I dared, gazing at her all the while until Anna gently lifted her out of my arms and she was gone. I thought my heart was going to break clean in two and I wondered what life was for if not to look after Elizabeth Nicole Burton, my beautiful baby girl. The nameless nurse returned and wheeled me back to the room of the 'girls like us'.

I lay in bed so very sad and lost, sore and completely empty without my baby. Then in walked Mum.

Having been informed that my labour had started the day after she left, she drove back to Leeds. All I wanted to do was pull the sheets over my head and hide from her and the world. Instead, I had to try and make small talk with her and that was the last thing I needed at that point in my life. Looking at her sitting there with the same cold expression on her face, I wondered how she felt about becoming a granny. I had nothing to say apart from to thank her for coming and it all sounded so false. She asked nothing about the birth of my baby or the name I had chosen. I knew she was glad it was all over, and new plans were afoot to get me home and back to school, back to normality and for me to get on with the rest of my life.

After Mum had gone, Anna popped in to say that Nicole was fast asleep in the nursery and she would be well looked after. 'I'll come back and see you as soon as I'm back on duty tonight,' she added, and she stroked my forehead before leaving the room.

'Thank you, Anna,' was all I could say. Then my thoughts shot straight back to Nicole.

I had often heard the babies crying in the nursery and thought how cruel it was to have them anywhere near us, but until giving birth to Nicole I did not understand just *how* cruel. Time and time again, I went to the toilets to read Bert's letters and heard muffled baby noises through the wall. After Nicole was born, I avoided going to the toilet until I was desperate. I even took to drinking less, hoping that was the solution. When I did go, I could not help listening and wondering which cry belonged to Nicole. There was one cry that always made my ears prick up, and I was convinced that was her.

The feeding routine in our room continued and this time it included me and my breasts. Just like the other girls, I fed perfect strangers' babies and there was no choice. All through feeding them, I avoided looking at them and pictured my baby girl instead which helped me to get through. One day, I almost let go of the baby I was feeding when another thought shot into my head. *Who on earth is feeding Nicole? Whose breast is she latching onto?*

I knew I would never find out and I felt myself sinking deeper down into the darkness of that dreadful place.

From my time in Falloden Nursing Home, I learned three lessons that have shaped the rest of my life.

If something hurts too much, switch off, be hard and repress your emotions – otherwise you will not be able to carry on. Blank the things that hurt you out of your mind. Only allow the memories to return once some kind of healing process is well underway, if that ever happens.

And never ever cry. All crying does is make your head thump and your eyes swell. It does not help one jot when your heart is breaking.

The final lesson was that on no account give all of your heart to anyone, ever again. They will always leave or be taken away. I can say that my real mum, my dad and Nicole had no choice, but part of working out what to do in the rest of my life came from those major life traumas I experienced. Going home to see Bert, I knew that part of me would be left in Leeds for good and he would never have all of my heart again. All this was hurting way too much for me to handle and I knew I would carry the mental and physical scars for the rest of my life. I was shattered and broken and, if the healing process ever came, it would take an eternity.

That evening, Anna came to see me as promised with an important piece of news. Thankfully, all the other girls were in the television room on the opposite side of the corridor so we could speak freely. She told me that she was leaving at the end of the week, on the same day I was due to go back home to Yarm. She had known this in the delivery room but, as they say, there is a time and a place for everything.

Now I understood how she found it in herself to allow me to cuddle Nicole. It was easy to talk to her and she trusted me enough to tell me the truth about her decision. She was going back to Ireland with no job prospects and her family was upset as she had been sending money back to them.

'I can't do this sort of thing any more. It's killing me watching the pain in you all.'

I understood what she meant, as she was far too kind and gentle a person to be delivering babies only for them to be taken away. Explaining further, she told me that her other role at Falloden was to assist a doctor downstairs to perform abortions. All manner of girls were brought over from Ireland as it was illegal to have abortions there. I was stunned that directly underneath our room for 'girls like us', there were girls whose chance of giving birth was being snatched away. Downstairs there would be discarded fetuses that had not had a chance of life as surely my baby would have ... somewhere. *After all, the first step is to be born, Nicole, and you've achieved that already,* I thought. The poor girls downstairs were being forced to end their babies' lives, we were upstairs being made to give our newborn babies away and it was all happening under one roof.

This place gets worse, I thought. *No wonder Anna's leaving. No wonder we all call it 'The Place from Hell'.*

Thank goodness I had met Anna. I loved talking to her and the closer it got to our leaving date, the more desperate I became to ask her for a special favour.

The next time I saw her, however, I had no time to ask anything as she rushed into our room, grabbed me by the arm and pulled me towards the door. She pointed to a smartly dressed couple who were walking along the corridor towards the nursery, accompanied by Mrs Lodge, the matron. All I could see was the back of them as they walked arm in arm. Anna whispered to me, 'That's them. They've come to see Nicole.'

I felt the blood draining from my face as it had on that first day at Falloden, and I watched them disappear into the nursery. Anna should never have told me in a million years, but she gave me the chance to lock their physical details into my memory bank. The lady was tall and blonde with a French pleat in her hair, just like Nina, the famous singer who sang with Frederick on *Top of the Pops* in the 1960s. Nina was pretty and her eyes smiled when she sang. She looked kind and I made myself believe this lady would be too. The lady's husband was tall and dark and that is all I can remember, apart from the fact that they looked well-to-do by the way they were dressed. Oh, how I hoped they would cherish my baby and let her be who she wanted to be as she grew up. Smile at her now and then and say, *'Girl, you done good.'*

Anna pulled me back into our room, whispering, 'They come from

Doncaster. She's a Methodist and he's a Jew. They've already got a three-year-old from here, called Christopher, so Nicole will have a big brother to play with. See … she'll be fine,' and she let go of my arm and cuddled me.

It was then I found the words to ask for my special favour, and having seen the couple going into the nursery it was more urgent than ever. 'Can I hold Nicole again before she goes?' I blurted out.

She stepped back and her eyes widened as she wondered how to answer. I quietly reminded her, 'You can't get sacked, Anna. You're already leaving.'

I felt guilty for involving her but the yearning to see Nicole again took over. After pacing up and down the room, she took both of my hands in hers and her blue eyes started to twinkle. Looking at me, she whispered, 'I'll think of something,' and off she went to do her job. I stood rooted to the spot fighting back the tears. Maybe, just maybe, there was going to be one more chance to see my baby girl.

The other three girls in the room for 'girls like us' left before me and we exchanged addresses with a promise to keep in touch. We never did. There was far too much sorrow in each of our hearts to ever meet again. We were so young and we had done our best to offer moral support during our time there. It had come naturally to us and we offered it with pleasure, to cope with the turmoil between us. To meet up again would bring the loss of our babies racing back to the forefront of our minds. None of us felt able to cope with that and we possibly never would. Each of us would spend the rest of our lives inwardly pining for our babies, and so we said our goodbyes with a false promise and I went back to our room alone.

After what seemed like days, Anna returned with her perfect plan.

'Following the evening feed, there's only one nurse who pops into the nursery every half hour to check on the babies. When the time is right, I'll come in here and wink at you. Go to the toilet and wait for a knock on the wall. That'll be your signal to come into the nursery.'

I was terrified and asked what would happen to her if we got caught. I can still see her determined look after all these years as she replied, 'I truly don't care, pet lamb. Just as you said, I'm leaving anyway.'

Three new girls had joined the 'girls like us' club in our shared room and, although I did my best to help them to settle in, I was not there long enough to get to know them. They were unaware that Nurse Anna and I shared confidences and plans, so it would be easy to pretend I was going to the toilet and then wait there until I heard a knock on the adjoining wall.

The penultimate day arrived and it dragged endlessly without any chores to do, without a radio to listen to or any magazines to read. All I could focus on was seeing Nicole again and Anna helping me to do it was beyond my wildest dreams. She popped in at various times on her shift, to practise the wink on me with a smile.

Then evening came. I sat watching the door from the corner of my eye, and as soon as Anna put her head round the door an unending shiver ran up and down my back, and my face started burning. Grabbing my wash bag, I slipped out of the room without saying anything to the new girls. I had been quiet since they arrived, withdrawing into myself, and only initiated conversation to help them settle in and put one cocky girl right on her voiced intention to break the rules while she was in Falloden.

My legs felt like jelly and my forehead broke out in a cold sweat as I made my way towards the bathroom with my heart pounding in my ears. The corridor seemed endless. Somehow I made it and rushed into a toilet cubicle, shut the door without a sound and waited for the knock with my breathing coming thick and fast. Every sound in the distance made me flinch and my pulse was racing. Suddenly, a sound nearby interrupted my thoughts.

There it was, the knock, and I knew I had to act immediately, or it would be too late. I grabbed my wash bag, opened the cubicle door and listened for any activity in the corridor. All was quiet. *Go … Go now,* I told myself, and I walked out watching and listening. Seconds elapsed, and I found myself inside the nursery with Anna standing by a cot in the middle row of the room. As I walked towards her, the other cots seemed to fade away and all I could see was my favourite nurse gently lifting my sleeping baby out of her cot. My heart was hammering as she passed Nicole to me, then it slowed as a calmness descended around us. I held her close, drinking in her features and petrified all the while that I would wake her. Her newborn smell surrounded me and love washed over me, bringing an ache to my throat. After a few precious minutes of closeness, Anna whispered, 'You need to go. I'll check the corridor's empty and when I tell you, you'll have to come quick.'

Those few seconds gave me time to say goodbye to Nicole forever. Cradling my baby girl for the last time, that first and last kiss on her sleeping brow is a treasured memory for me and I hope for her too. Somehow, I knew I would see her again. Words I wanted to whisper were hard to say for the lump aching so powerfully in my throat. I managed to blink away the tears and murmured my final words.

'I'll always be with you, no matter where we both are. No matter what happens, one day I'll find you. I love you, Nicole. See you soon,' and that was it. My whole world had just ended. Hopefully, Nicole's was just about to begin.

That night I lay awake for hours, listening for the sound of my baby crying and knowing that if I heard her, I would have to go, not caring that there may be a nurse there. I was also wondering if I dare sneak back along to the nursery just to have another look at her. All the while, my tears flowed endlessly, and my head was thumping because I had not become hard enough to carry out the lesson that Falloden had taught me.

I was sobbing so hard I could hardly breathe, because in my heart I knew I could not go back to see her ever again. Nurse Anna had trusted me, as I had trusted her, and that trust between us must always remain.

After a while, my strength returned and I calmed myself down. All the other girls were fast asleep and I lay in that terrible place quietly singing. Ever so quietly, I sang every word of the song destined to be the song for Nicole. I hoped she could hear me and carry that song with her throughout life, knowing that I loved her completely.

I sang it without crying until the last few lines faded into racking sobs once more. Of course, unlike in the lyrics of 'Your Song', I would never forget whether her eyes were green or blue. Day after day, those beautiful blue eyes were right there with me. Each time I closed my eyes at night, I saw them, and I whispered to her, 'Yours are the sweetest eyes I've ever seen.'

Thank you, Elton John, for writing such an emotional song in the year my baby was born. Goodnight and God Bless, Nicole.

The next morning, my eyes were swollen to mere slits and my face was puffy and tight as I packed for my escape from Falloden Nursing Home.

I expected to feel a sense of relief and freedom as I walked out of the front door, leaving 'The Place From Hell', but neither feeling was there. All I could think of was my baby and, if I did not put into action 'the blanking out things that hurt' lesson soon, I knew I would crumble and my heart would wither away. I made sure I saw two people in the 'place without smiles' before my escape. My special nurse Anna of course, and Beryl the cook-cum-general-kitchen-hand who helped me get through the early weeks at Falloden. Other goodbyes were said out of politeness and expectation from the person I had grown to despise.

I saw her orange Mini appear from the shadows around ten o'clock and, with my suitcase and medication packed, as well as all of Bert's love letters, I pulled on my purple platform boots to prove to myself that I really was leaving 'The Place From Hell'. I got in the car, staring straight ahead, and Mum drove off back towards Yarm and the prison called 'home'.

As she drove out through the tunnel of despair, I sat there unable to believe what she had forced me to do and surrounded by a new kind of grief, knowing that each mile was taking me further away from Nicole. I still believed she could not be so cruel, that she would relent and turn her car around. Each roundabout, each set of traffic lights, lessened any hope of that, and I withdrew once again after flinging more bricks onto *The Wall Against Mum.*

Once out of Leeds my thoughts were interrupted with talk of getting back to school as quickly as possible, 'It's for the best, Anne. A week at home then back to school. It'll take your mind off things.'

'Things?' I thought. *What do you mean ... 'things?' Why can't you even say the words?*

What a way to talk. It was what Mum had always done: spoken without any emotion and without a single scrap of love for me. *Why bring up all these plans when you know my heart's breaking? Can't you just hold me and hug me, and tell me that everything'll be alright? Or just leave me alone ... I hate you! ... There now, I've said it.*

The trouble was, I had not uttered a single word. I would never dare. I was so scared of her. I had to do as she said and she knew that. I had spent all of my life being controlled, and I wanted to take control of my own life from that day forward but had no idea how to achieve that wish. All I knew was that I was not a little girl any more and I had just proved that.

Living with you again is going to be hell, I thought as we headed home. *Where, oh where, is my real Mum?* She would have held me and hugged me, I was sure, until I remembered that I had been given away too. Were we both so weak that we could not stand up to anyone?

Once again Mum interrupted my thoughts, 'I've made an appointment tomorrow afternoon for you at Dr Fraser's and you'll be going on the pill.

We want no more of this nonsense, do we?'

I did not answer because I would have screamed at her to shut up and no doubt have sworn at her. Again and again. I would have exploded. Instead I thought, *I don't want an appointment. I didn't ask for an appointment so how can you say* you've *made it for* me. *For you, you mean. I'm not allowed to see Bert anyway, am I? So why do I have to go on the pill?*

Her voice piped up with words that made me wonder if, as well as controlling me, she could read my mind, 'As soon as the pill's working, I'll think about letting you see Bert again because I know you'll find a way. You always have.'

And that was that. Silence ruled the rest of our journey home.

('Your Song' – Elton John – 1971)

('Shout to the Top' – Style Council – 1984)

The Shell

Walking wounded we

Our inexpressible pain hidden deep within

The passing pains of childbirth supplanted

By the unending pain of separation, a life sentence

Murderers receive time-limited sentences

But we who gave life, get no remission

And so I walk and talk and work and smile

And nobody would guess the despair within

Or that I feel like a life-size mechanical doll

Hollow inside, like an empty shell.

19

On Being Back Home

On that first night back home, I tossed and turned trying to eradicate the nightmare of Falloden from my thoughts. Each time I closed my eyes, Nicole's newborn face came flying towards me, reminding me that I had abandoned her. Intermittently sleeping throughout, I woke up sobbing with my body drenched in sweat, and the Falloden nightmare continued as a reality in the darkness of my room.

By the morning I was exhausted and had to heave my post-pregnancy body out of bed before I succumbed to sorrow completely. I wished I could ignore the day and hide away from the world. I had no chance of that. By nine o'clock, Mum struck up the hoover with its familiar whining tune, reminding me it was time to rise and shine.

Rise and shine? I thought. *I'll never shine again.*

In the afternoon, Mum drove me down to Yarm and parked up on the cobbles. 'I'll meet you here in half an hour and mind you come straight back.'

Letting me go to the doctors by myself was a first for her, and my surprise must have shown. 'If you're old enough to have a baby, you're old enough to ask for the pill yourself. Anyway, he knows you're coming. Go on then, off you go,' and with that command we went our separate ways.

Maybe she doesn't want to be seen with me in the High Street? I thought, and rushed, head down, towards the surgery.

Sitting in the waiting room, generating an aura of shame and embarrassment, I fidgeted with my nails to avoid eye contact with anyone. I knew all the other patients by sight, and of course I knew the receptionist who had been there for donkey's years and seen me growing up. I felt all eyes focusing on my stomach and wondered if they all knew what I had done, even though I had been banished to Leeds so that they would not.

Eventually, I was called into Doctor Fraser's surgery and the aura of shame and embarrassment followed me through his door. He too remembered me as a child, playing in his house with his daughter, Anita, and eating as a welcome part of their family, after sliding down their wonderful banisters to reach the dining room. He would also remember coming to our house and rushing straight past me on that fateful night to do his best for my dad. Now I was just a young girl who had chosen the wrong path in life and I would surely never be welcome again in his house – or indeed anywhere in Yarm.

Doctor Fraser's attitude surprised me. He looked up as I entered and a smile crossed his face as he pointed to a chair opposite him. I sat down, not knowing what to say. His deep Irish lilt broke the ice.

'Well, good afternoon, Anne Burton. It's nice to have you back in Yarm. I know it's been hard for you since your dad died and I understand how you must be feeling. It all takes time. As far as the other thing's concerned, it's all over now,' then he added, 'It'll take time as well, you know.' I couldn't believe his kindness towards me.

He examined me to make sure all my working parts were in order and then struck up a conversation about the pill and its side effects. He made it clear I needed to take it religiously each day, otherwise I may become pregnant again if I was to continue with sexual adventures. He talked to me as an adult in his matter-of fact-way, and I sat, head up, listening to his advice. Handing me a post-dated prescription, he explained that my body needed to heal completely for the next five weeks before starting to take the tablets.

As I got up to leave, he said, 'Good luck back at school, Anne, and give my regards to your mother,' and off I went, stunned that someone had treated me like a human being. Mum was nowhere to be seen when I got back to the car and I spent the next quarter of an hour doing my best to remain invisible, standing in Yarm High Street waiting for her.

On her return, she said, 'It took longer than I thought,' and flung her shopping bag on the back seat before letting me into the car.

'Hurry up and get in then. What did Doctor Fraser say?'

'It'll be five weeks until I can get it. My body has to heal.'

Reversing the car, she glared at me saying, 'So Bert will have to wait … to see you, I mean.'

Focussing straight ahead, I nodded. *We'll see about that*, I thought.

The weekend arrived and I lay in bed staring blankly at the walls of my bedroom, which I'd decorated soon after moving from the shop. Three walls were covered in red swirly pop-art-type wallpaper and I had painted the wall above my bed in plain white, waiting for an idea to flourish. Allowing me my own choice of wallpaper for the first time, Mum told me I was a Bohemian when she saw what I picked, and after I asked what it meant, she explained with a sneer that I was ahead of my time with my creative ideas, as if that was wrong.

Dejected and sad, my head was exploding with thoughts of Bert and Nicole, and I knew a gigantic sketch needed to fill that white wall pretty soon, to take away the blankness and emptiness it held as it echoed exactly how I was feeling. Inspiration was yet to come but something had to be done to fix both the wall and myself. For the whole weekend, I took refuge in my room and drew sketches of the plans for my white wall. I was trying to move on and distract myself but failing miserably. One after another, I scratched the sketches out – still searching for an idea – and the pencils lay silent and still, waiting.

My friends rang to welcome me home, saying they had asked Mum if they could visit but permission had been refused. Our conversations were stilted and false as they could be heard all over the house and I knew Mum had an ear cocked, somewhere. So, when Pauline rang and put Bert on, I was flabbergasted and did not know what to say. Bert calmly took over. 'I'll be under 'our' tree at seven o'clock on Monday night. Just say you're going for a walk like you've always done. If she won't let you, I'll be back in touch,' and he signed off by saying, 'I love you.'

I melted, hearing his voice say those words to me. I knew he meant it. Then he passed me back to Pauline. The two of us carried on chatting as if nothing had happened. She told me she was going to our favourite dancing place, The Kirk, that night, and I was so jealous. We talked for a while longer then the pips went, signalling the end of her call, and she hung up.

Mum asked what Pauline had said. As soon as I mentioned The Kirk, I imagined Mum's swift retort, even before it came, because it was always the same. She proved me right by saying, 'They say there are drugs there. It's a den of iniquity.'

After the weekend, Mum went to work as usual and I stayed in my room with the emptiness and grief engulfing me. Gingerly looking in the mirror at my body without a baby, I still looked pregnant and did not understand why. I looked disgusting and I had nothing to show for it. Just a fat stomach covered in bright red, almost luminescent scars, and above it, invisible to the world, a heart cracked wide open. Looking away, my thoughts switched to Bert and although I was longing to see him under 'our' tree, I knew he had already lost a part of me. Until Nicole was born and became a real human being, I loved Bert completely because when she was still inside me, she was not yet a true part of my life. Once born and touched and held by me, if only for a few precious seconds, she became the biggest part of my life; which made me unsure how to be with Bert again, as it was in the old days of Bert and Anne, and how to carry on as if nothing had changed.

With my radio blaring, I attacked the white wall. The sketching pencils took control and the sorrow flew down the lead and leapt out, producing a three-foot face that was mine. A face split down the middle by a dark, jagged crack. One side of the face was lightly shaded, had an eye that shone bright and a mouth tilting upwards. She was perfect. The other side was darker with an expressionless eye gazing into the distance, as if searching for something, and had a straight mouth, clamped tight shut. It held little emotion, but running down her cheek was a solitary tear. The whole face was framed with a shoulder-length bob and a fringe, just like mine.

I stood back with my pencils in hand, in disbelief. Something had willed me on and guided me to the end. Something had taken me over and driven me without stopping. Perhaps it was my soul pouring out the unbearable pain and helping me to carry on. Whatever it was, that drawing watched over me night after night and I thanked it for helping me to forget for a while.

When Mum saw it her eyes narrowed, and her mouth began to form angry words which never came. Words demanding to know how I dare draw on my wall. Instead of saying anything, she stared at the face, glared at me and walked out of my room.

After dinner, we were back in the kitchen with the usual routine of, 'I'll wash, you dry and put away.' The same old, same old, same. *How much longer do I have to be trapped here with you?* I thought.

I wanted to scream in her face, tell her how cruel she was and break out of the house and bolt towards another life, but I failed to even find the courage on that Monday evening to say I was going for a walk. So if Bert was there, under 'our' tree, he was there alone.

'The Face' – amazingly replicated in 2022, by twelve-year-old Alabama Rose Watson and used with complete gratitude.

~ 229 ~

Mum and I watched television in silence. I felt suffocated being in the same room as her and said, 'I'm going upstairs to read.'

'Why don't you bring your book down? You can read here.'

No way, I thought. If that was an attempt at an apology it had not worked. Politely, I explained that I needed to lie flat as my stitches inside me were agony, and she let me go.

Tuesday dawned, which meant Mum would be going to her Women's Institute meeting – unless, of course, she had been demoted from being President, all because of me … She did go, and in my first week back home she resumed all her evening activities, leaving me at home alone again, surrounded by my sorrow and grief with only 'Dad's cloud' to keep me company. I went to 'our' tree and hung about but no one came. I pinned a message on it in case Bert came by while walking Brig, his black Labrador. 'I'll be here at 7 o'clock tomorrow,' was all it said.

The following evening the message had gone. My insecurity kicked in. *Has Bert seen the message and ignored it? Has the message blown off? So, where's the drawing pin?* I hunted for both on the ground but could see neither. My trust and faith in Bert were at an all-time low. I found myself thinking of the Falloden lesson and swore to abide by it: *don't give all of your heart to anyone.* I went home and did not cry.

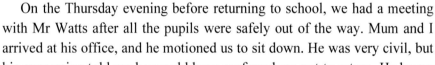

On the Thursday evening before returning to school, we had a meeting with Mr Watts after all the pupils were safely out of the way. Mum and I arrived at his office, and he motioned us to sit down. He was very civil, but his expression told me he would have preferred me not to return. He began by reminding me that 'the story' of my absence must be upheld and only told if necessary.

Then he moved on to say that, while I was in Leeds, he had chosen the prefects for the term ahead and with being absent I had missed out on the chance. I could not believe it. All through my six years at that school, I held one simple wish: to become a prefect, wear a badge and feel proud – but it was not to be. On my first day back, everyone in the class was sporting their shiny 'Prefect' badge on their lapels, apart from me. It was an indirect way of singling me out and punishing me without a word.

Mr Watts continued, telling me I was banned from leaving the school premises at lunchtime, a privilege given to all sixth form pupils. This ban would last until the end of term when he would review it. Once again, I was gutted. Before going to Leeds, I was already in the lower sixth, and Pauline and I had often signed out of school at lunchtimes to rush to Spark's bakery on the High Street, to buy ourselves a treat. School rules stated that eating on the street was expressly forbidden, and we abided by them and took our food back to school. On other occasions, we pushed our luck and signed out with the purpose of meeting Bert on the riverbank by the Methodist chapel during his half-hour lunch break.

Lunchtime freedom and meeting Bert were a thing of the past. Even worse, was that everyone else in school would eventually question why I was being punished. Punished for Mum being ill? I don't think so. Glancing at Mum during that meeting with Mr Watts, it was like 'Falloden revisited'. She wore the same smug expression as at the Falloden 'interview' and instantly I knew that Mr Watts had let her in on the agenda of the meeting beforehand. She was learning to be more deceitful than me. Walking away from our meeting, I was already dreading my first day back.

('Baby Come Back' – The Equals – 1968)

('Reason to Believe' – Rod Stewart – 1971)

20

On Being Back at School

Imagining the multitude of grim scenarios awaiting me, after I walked through those school gates on my first day back, led to another night of full-blown nightmares and drenched sheets. The weekend before, I tried on my school skirt and blouse, which were still as tight as when I had been six months pregnant but arriving in new clothes would have looked a trifle fishy. At least the weather was cool, so my red baggy school jumper helped me to hide my post-birth shape. I decided to shed 'My Protector', the black duffle coat that had camouflaged my shameful secret from everyone at school for six months before the birth of Nicole. Now she was gone and all I had left of her was the constant ache in my heart and the slash of angry scars across my belly. The last time I had walked along the corridors of Yarm Grammar School she was as close as she could be, safe in my womb.

Monday morning dawned and I was hoping that Mum might offer me a lift on that first day back, but I was told, 'Things'll look strange if I drop you off. You'll have to walk.' '*Things'. There's that word again,* I thought.

I planned to be one of the first at school and set off as soon as Mum left for work. As she walked out, she bluntly reminded me of 'the story' to be told and that explanations were unnecessary unless asked outright. Then she was gone, slamming the front door behind her.

'Good luck,' I called, staring at the front door and wondering why she was unable to bring herself to say that to me.

I slung my old school haversack over one shoulder, locked the door and started walking. Having spent a whole week at home after returning from Falloden, I thought I would be strong enough, both mentally and physically, for that first walk back to school. I was so wrong. Walking down Urlay Nook Road towards Yarm, the memories came flooding back, tormenting me. Bert had walked me home so many times up that road and here I was walking down it, utterly alone. I had walked up and down to school and back for six months with Nicole growing inside me, and now I was empty and broken without her.

On that Monday morning, I put one foot in front of the other and, thinking of the Falloden lesson, I fought back the tears. Down the bank past The Blue Bell and across the bridge that led into Yarm. I could almost hear the Blue Bell juke box blasting out our favourite songs, and wondered if the vehicles passing me by were full of passengers gawking at me and saying to each other, 'There's Anne Burton. She got pregnant, you know. Wonder what happened to it?' I kept my eyes focused straight ahead.

I began to wonder if anyone had pointed a finger at Bert while I was away, with people saying to each other, 'There's Bert Lamplugh. He's the one who got Anne Burton pregnant.'

It was always the girl's fault in other people's minds, when most of us did not have a clue what we were doing or the implications of doing it. And the boys carried on regardless. By the time all these thoughts had raced through my head, I was walking past our old shop, and I longed to be a little girl again skipping beside my dad.

I turned towards our old front door and whispered, 'Hello Dad. I still miss you so much,' and swallowed the lump forming in my throat.

Gritting my teeth, I struggled up The Spital towards the turn-off for the school bank with the raw scars down below viciously rubbing together with each agonising step. I couldn't slow down for fear of raising suspicion, so I soldiered on. Another lesson learned in life. Soldier on until you can soldier on no more. As I turned the corner to go up Grammar School bank,

I spotted Bob the caretaker unlocking the school gates. Being early I thought I would have avoided him. I was mortified and hesitated wondering whether to backtrack, but he spotted me. He waved and that gave me confidence to wave back and carry on as best I could.

As I approached him, I was waiting for the inevitable greeting of, 'Good morning, Miss Pea,' but it never came. Instead, he glanced left and right to make sure no one was watching and then gave me a gentle hug. 'Welcome back,' he said – and added, 'Miss Pea.'

He smiled, watching me as I passed him, and I managed to smile back. *Thank you, Bob*, I thought. I made straight for the toilet block which was just by the school gates, to check I was not bleeding, and then realised I did not know what to do or where to go next. I wanted the ground to swallow me up and bury my shame at the same time. There were a few pupils already milling about, so for normality's sake I decided to go into 'The Den' which was designated for sixth formers only. It was on the ground floor of an old Victorian building, right next to Mr Watts's office where our meeting had been the week before, and upstairs were the sixth form classrooms. An early equivalent of a sixth form block, I suppose.

'The Den' was a place of our own with a kettle and a fridge stuffed full of cans of pop, Coca-Cola and people's packed lunches. Two old sofas had been donated by some parents, a big square table and four dining chairs too. Permitted posters of pop stars lined the walls. Behind 'The Den' was another room, complete with table tennis table, and a smelly passage leading to the 'smokers' yard' – to which most teachers turned a blind eye. As sixth formers, we had gone up in the world. No more diving behind the bike sheds for us at breaktimes and being offered a puff on a cigarette from the boys for a sneaky look down our blouses.

Going into 'The Den', I made a beeline for the kettle and faced the wall to avoid any eye contact or conversation with other sixth formers trooping in.

I think everyone knew why I had been absent but nothing was said. When the bell for lessons rang, I was confronted by a classmate called Sian as we all piled into the English room upstairs. She was a short, dark-haired, freckle-faced Welsh girl with bandy legs and a sharp tongue in her mouth, and we had never really hit it off. In a very loud voice she said, 'You're back then. Did you have twins?'

Blushing furiously, I looked straight at her, keeping my voice in check, and replied, 'No, it was triplets actually,' which made everyone snigger – and not at me. She never asked again.

Settling back into school was as dreadful as I had imagined. I withdrew into a world of my own again, intent on ignoring the knowing looks from fellow pupils and staff. I was consumed by sorrow just like when my dad had died, but this was different. The person I had lost this time around was very much alive. I just did not know where she was. I felt sorrow, mixed with shame which was highlighted by everyone's attitude towards me. I was ashamed to be me. The wariness everyone showed when engaging with me convinced me even more than before that I was not worth bothering with. When I say 'everyone', that is not quite true. My friends stood by me as only true friends do, and for that I am eternally grateful. Without their support I am sure I would have gone under altogether.

There was another sector at school that continued to find me acceptable to talk to, and that was some of the older boys. They obviously thought, in their teenage wisdom, that having been pregnant meant I must be 'a goer', 'an easy lay', and that was worth its weight in gold at their age, so they continued trying to flirt with me. In their eyes I had an added advantage. I was 'a goer' with the biggest breasts in school. I was not interested. I was still Bert's girl.

So why hasn't he tried to get in touch with me? I asked myself. I didn't understand.

The following week he rang Pauline's house. He explained to her that he thought it was better to leave it for a while, for me to settle back into school and give Mum time to calm down. Of course, I did not believe all that. I believed he was looking for an easy way out as he had not cared enough in the first place, had he? Or, maybe he was timing our reconciliation to coincide with me starting to take the pill. Reports of him walking along the High Street with other girls were still rife and were coming at me from every angle. I did not know who to believe.

Defensively, I brought the hatred in my heart to the forefront. It was my only chance of dealing with the desolation that was consuming me like a tidal wave and pulling me under, time after time. With that new-found hatred and the secret strength it offered me to survive, I dragged myself to school each day feeling stronger but still numb. Numb to the point that I withdrew further and became like a zombie. Often my friends had to repeat their questions as I was in another world, dreaming of what might have been before the hatred kicked in. I was in 'Nicole and Bert' world and teetering on the edge of a precipice.

Fortunately for me, I hovered on the edge and did not jump, as two weeks later my life took a turn for the better. Bert knocked on our door to seek permission from Mum to see me again. Mum and Bert. Face to face, again. That was brave, as the last time it had happened was the announcement of my pregnancy. My hatred evaporated as I listened from the landing, but I was so mixed up I was unsure I wanted to go back to where we had left off. As usual Mum took over. She called me down from my bedroom, demanding a solemn promise from both of us that any kind of 'hanky panky' would be avoided. Of course, we both instantly nodded our heads in agreement. The five weeks was nearly up and, while we stood there sheepishly, Mum worked out the date when I could start on the pill, right there, in front of us both, by calculating it on her fingers. How embarrassing was that?

An initial date was set for Bert to come and collect me for our first evening back together. Since returning home from Leeds, Mum must have noticed how sad and withdrawn I was, even if she chose to ignore it, and I suppose she hoped that was to do with Bert. So letting Bert see me again would fettle that sadness for once and for all, in her head. Then *'things'* would get back to normal. I would buckle down and pass my 'A' levels and become the perfect teacher and finally become the perfect daughter she so wanted. I stood there wanting to scream at each of them in turn. *Why don't you ask me what* I *want to do? Why would I want to see* you *again when you've let our baby go?*

I had to admit it would be good to spend time with Bert again even if it felt wrong, so I kept my thoughts to myself, but my emotions were on the biggest rollercoaster ride ever and I had no control over them.

On that first evening back together, and over the next few weeks, we carried on with our pre-Leeds lifestyle. Five days a week Bert went to work, as before. Five days a week I went to school, as before. We were together, either with permission from Mum or in secret when Mum was out. We went for walks by the river and long drives in his car which still proudly displayed both our names on its wings. We returned to the Blue Bell, our favourite pub, and everyone accepted without question that Bert and Anne were back together.

Bert was the same kind and gentle person with the same bright, blue eyes that twinkled only for me. We kissed and cuddled under 'our' tree and it was beautiful to be together once more. We walked and talked and laughed without making any plans this time around. We pulled up in country lay-bys desperate to prove that the pill was doing its job, holding each other so close and wrapped around each other just like in the old days. We drank and listened to music with friends in our local pubs, and all was well, or so Bert obviously thought. Deep in my soul something had changed.

My heart was broken and my sparkle had gone, left in Leeds along with Nicole.

Bert found it easy to carry on as before without ever thinking to ask about the ache in my heart. I took to drinking more and more, as alcohol took the pain away and helped me to believe things were 'All Right Now', just like Free had said, but in my young heart I knew it was simply untrue. My feelings for Bert were changing. The faith had gone and all that was left was the hope I could get through all this. I could not understand how he could carry on as if Nicole did not matter, as if she had never existed. I tried to tell myself it was because I had carried her inside me for a full nine months, and that it was different for him, which explained why he did not seem to be hurting at all. With every date, something verging on the hatred I'd felt was building up inside me again and I was unable to shake it off. I wanted to run away from the sadness but it followed me everywhere, like a storm waiting to break. *Soldier on,* I told myself.

In the January of 1972, I turned eighteen. Being eighteen meant many things became legal for me. I could vote. I could legally go to pubs. I could go legally to The Kirk. It was a special birthday, and teenagers in the '70s chose whether to celebrate it as a marker of adulthood or wait three more years and celebrate being twenty-one. Mum asked me which I wanted to do and my decision was immediate. I would wait. What was there to celebrate about being eighteen? There was no General Election that year to cast a vote. I had been going into pubs and to *The Kirk* since I was fifteen so nothing would change there either.

Most importantly, with Nicole's first birthday coming up, celebrating was the last thing on my mind. That was the only milestone I constantly thought about. Nearly a whole year had passed since I had held her in my arms for those precious few minutes. The memories of her special smell and the softness of her baby skin came rushing back to me most nights in devastating dreams. Why the hell would I want an eighteenth birthday party, pretending to be happy and carefree, surrounded by relatives who had predicted, long ago, that Anne – the adopted one – would bring shame to the family. *Bad blood.* I could almost hear them saying, 'We told Margaret and Sandy, but they would not listen.'

Instead of a party, Bert and I went to the Blue Bell, with Mum's permission of course. My birthday fell on a Wednesday and as going out on a school night was still unheard of, we had to wait until the weekend. Instead of relatives, I was surrounded by people of my own age doing the things we had done for years. Putting precious coins in the juke box to hear our favourite songs, smoking cigarettes enveloped by a blue fog and chatting together. The drinks were flowing that night. Bert bought me a Snowball, which was a mixture of advocaat and lemonade, followed by a Babycham, and then I graduated onto gin and tonics. I could feel the drink-induced happiness of being eighteen starting to course through me.

Suddenly, all went deathly quiet as the door to the back room swung open and two uniformed police officers strode in. One male, one female. Just like the police dramas on television, the female police officer was as smart as a dart, with swept-up, backcombed, blonde hair, half hidden by her police hat, and an immaculate uniform with legs covered in sheer black stockings. There were no identity cards back then to prove anyone's age, merely teenagers hoping they looked grown-up enough to be in the pub. I had looked about twelve for many years after I was twelve, and still looked way under eighteen. That night, however, I willed them to come over to me and they did as their first port of call.

'And how old are you then, young lady?' the policeman enquired.

Usually being so quiet and reserved, I even shocked myself when I stood up from my seat to answer, and fuelled by alcohol, declared in a loud voice, 'I'm eighteen, officer, and it's my birthday today,' and exploded into a fit of giggles.

All those years of going into the Blue Bell and this was the first time the police had ever set foot in the place in our presence. I was excited that they had come on my eighteenth birthday and more exciting was that I could tell the truth. I had nothing to fear. They believed me, or chose not to follow it up, and moved on to question other drinkers in the back room. It was part of their duty in the 1970s, a formality to carry out, but no one was asked to leave, even though we knew there were some fellow drinkers who were underage, carefully lying their heads off. You could feel the relief permeate the room when they left, as most of us respected the police and thought of them as an authority to be listened to rather than to be ridiculed, as nowadays.

I was extremely tiddly when Bert walked me home on that birthday night, and we stopped off at the entrance to the boiler house of 'The Comp' for another chance to prove the worth of the pill. Only yards away from my house. What an exciting night it had been, but I still found it so hard to look into those blue eyes of his without the hurt grabbing me deep down inside. As I walked up the drive towards home, he blew me a kiss and said, 'Happy birthday, Maggie May, I love you'.

The next two months saw a big, black cloud hovering over my head as Nicole's first birthday approached. I lay in bed at night and planned what I would have done for her. There would have been chains of paper streamers all across the ceiling, and coloured balloons and as many presents as I could muster. Presents meant for boys as well as for girls, unlike my childhood days. A home-made cake – not that I had ever baked a cake in my life – but it would have been time to learn. It would have been the best day of her life so far.

In reality, all I could do was hope and pray that, somewhere, someone was planning all these treats to give her a wonderful first birthday, filled with love and happiness, and that her first year had been a perfect one. I prayed she was not surrounded by relatives looking at her as if she had two heads and that instead she had already been accepted as a special baby and not just as one of the 'adopted' variety, like me. All those thoughts, feelings and dreams, I experienced alone. I was unable to find a way to talk to Bert about how I was feeling and there was no way Mum would have listened. She would have brushed it all aside and told me to 'snap out of it'. My friends had their own lives and I hardly ever opened up to them either. No one understood and no one ever could, especially as no one ever knew how I was feeling. It was bottled up inside me like a huge fuse waiting to be lit. An explosion waiting to happen.

School seemed to be endless in that year of 1972, without any purpose whatsoever. I lost all interest in working towards my 'A' levels which were coming up in May, even though I had surprisingly passed the three 'O' level resits taken in Leeds with Mum and Auntie Dorothy sternly invigilating. Back at school, anyone wishing to apply to teacher training college had already received guidance from careers officers, as college interviews were also to be held in the month of May. I knew I did not want to go, but there was no option. Once again, my future had been controlled by Mum. I played the game and filled in my application forms to the best of my ability, as even though I had no interest I knew I had to do something with the rest of my life. Having read all the prospectuses and understanding little of what they were offering, I opted to choose by location – even though I was unsure where any of the locations were – and did not really care.

Northumberland College of Education in the village of Ponteland, nine miles north of the City of Newcastle, was my first choice for some reason. My second choice was Brighton and my third, Tooting, near London. All strange names to me but any place had to be better than living with Mum. Even the thought of moving away from Bert sometimes seemed like a good idea. It would hopefully distance me from the memories that were so full on in my own hometown, and if that didn't work at least it would be a new start. Something to focus on and try to forget for a while. I was trying to think positive, but the big black cloud was always there, right above me, hovering. In fact, my skies were full of clouds now that 'Nicole's cloud' had joined the 'adoption cloud' and 'Dad's cloud' too. I hardly ever managed to spot the sun.

The week before Nicole's first birthday in 1972, Bert's brother Howard married Cynthia from Aline's, and I do not remember the day at all even though the photo below proves I was there. Eleven months after Nicole's birth and I was still reeling in my own world of numbness and sorrow.

Bert and I, second and third from left.
Christine – Bert's late sister, to the left of us.
Howard and Cynthia with their wedding day smiles.
(Note the purple 'Escape from Falloden' platform boots).

A month and a half after the wedding, I was invited for an interview at my first choice of college in Ponteland and, for a moment, I felt proud. Having passed eight 'O' levels in total meant I was eligible for a place without waiting for my 'A' level results. Three years of further study sounded like an awful long time, and I was quite shocked to get an interview. Maybe it was because 'being pregnant at sixteen' was not included on my list of qualifications. This was the chance of a new beginning, and I knew I had to take it.

The interview day came and went, and a month after travelling up to Newcastle by train, a large brown envelope lay waiting for me on the mat inside our front door when I got back from school one day. It had the Northumberland College of Education logo stamped firmly in one corner and my heart skipped a beat. *What if I've been accepted?* I thought, followed closely by ... *what if I've been refused?*

I was at a crossroads in my life and was scared which path the letter was going to direct me along. Gingerly, I opened the envelope and slowly pulled out the headed notepaper far enough to see the first couple of lines, which read, 'We are pleased to inform you that your interview has been successful. Margaret Anne Burton is offered a place on our Certificate of Education course beginning in October 1972 ...'

Well, there you are, I thought, *you did it!* Straight away Mum came into the equation. *Now will she finally be proud of me?* I wondered.

When I showed her the letter and she took it all in, the expression fleeting across her face was one of total relief and I knew she could not wait to get rid of me. Surprisingly, she drew me towards her for a few seconds and gave me a hug, then pushed me back to arm's length. Still no words like, 'Well done!' Maybe I had been wrong all those years. Maybe words like those were only said in films or on the television. *Dad used to say those words though,* I thought, *so it still must happen in families.*

I stood there in the hall with her, waiting for more but nothing came. She kept her eyes glued to the letter as if she could not believe I was going.

After what seemed like ages, and to alleviate the situation, I summoned up the courage to ask her if she was proud of me. She looked at me with pain in her eyes, obviously wondering how to reply, and simply offered the words, 'It'll do us both good, Anne.'

My moment of pride was snatched away, and I knew whatever I did in life from now on, I would never be forgiven for becoming pregnant and putting shame on her and the rest of the family.

('No Matter What' – Badfinger – 1970)

('Maggie May' – Rod Stewart and The Faces – 1971)

('Won't Get Fooled Again' – The Who – 1971)

('It's Too Late' – Carole King – 1971)

21

My Escape Route

Bert took me in his arms when I told him about my offer of a place at college. We clung on to each other, knowing that I would be going away again for a much longer time, and the cuddle said it all. He was frightened of losing me.

For the next few weeks, I saw much less of him as my time was taken up with forced revision for my 'A' levels. The dining room in our house became the revision room, where each evening, Monday to Friday, I sat at the table piled high with school books trying to take in and retain all the facts needed to pass my exams. Mum relented and allowed me to have Radio 1 playing quietly in the background. For years before – apart from in Leeds – permission had been denied with the words, 'You can't possibly learn with all that music playing,' and I was told to switch the radio off. I tried to explain that it helped me to concentrate but to no avail. This time around, she must have realised that her years of control were nearly over and gave in. I did my best to focus, but I wanted to be out and about with Bert even though I was not sure about him any more.

I've already got a place at college so what's the point of all this? I wondered, trying my best to revise. When the weekends arrived, I was allowed out.

One particular weekend, I broached an idea to Bert which I had been mulling over during the week, head supposedly in my school books.

A music festival in Lincoln was on for four days during the Spring Bank Holiday. It was called The Great Western Express Festival, and for only £4.50 we would get to see famous bands such as *Nazareth, Don McLean* and *The Faces,* led by my all-time musical hero *Rod Stewart.* I explained that my exams would be over by then and this would be the last opportunity to do something together before I went off to college.

'It'll be a change of scenery for us, and it might take our minds off Nicole for a while,' I said, imploring him to think about it.

He listened and then the questions started to flow.

'What will you tell your Mum? She won't let you go to a festival with me, will she? How're we going to get there? … where will we sleep?' The practical questions kept rolling off his tongue. Obstacle after obstacle, but I knew I had to get away.

'Oh, come on Bert. Let's do something different for once!'

I suggested a plan. 'I'll ask Sue if I can 'stay' at her house. It's worked before hasn't it?'

Bert agreed but said he could only ask for the Friday off work and so we made a plan to hitch a lift down that day and a lift back on the Monday, to be ready for his work and my school the following day. I didn't know what we could sleep in so suggested that two black bin bags would have to do, explaining,

'Other people sleep in bin bags at festivals. I've seen them on the television.'

He looked at me as if I was mad, but he softened when I reminded him it would be our last adventure together for the foreseeable future.

'Alright then. I'll ask for time off and see what they say,' and he wrapped his arms around me. At least it was a plan, and I was desperate for it to work. In the meantime, it was something to get excited about and something to divert our minds away from all the chaos in our lives.

We arranged to meet under 'our' tree the following Tuesday, and by then Bert would have an answer to his request for time off work and I would know if Sue had agreed to let me 'stay' at her house. The following Monday at school, she agreed straight away as she owed me a favour from a few weeks before when she had 'stayed' at my house.

As soon as Mum left for her Women's Institute meeting, I raced round the corner to 'our' tree and Bert and Brig were already there. Bert was grinning from ear to ear and I knew that his request for time off had been granted. On top of that, his older brother Howard had offered to drive us as far as the Newark roundabout on the A1, and we would be able to hitch a lift from there to the festival. He was off work that Friday too and so it all fitted in.

There was only one stumbling block before our planned adventure. The dreaded 'A' level exams. I had revised like billy-o for the couple of weeks before they began, but still without any real interest in passing. A full week of exams followed and then they were behind me. After that final exam, I heaved a huge sigh of relief as I put my pen down and handed in my French paper to the invigilator. I was free. *Totalement libre.* For a while …

Walking home, I started daydreaming about our forthcoming festival adventure and hoped Bert and I could enjoy our time together. I knew our relationship had changed dramatically and that maybe we should not be going at all. We were scarred by a part of our young lives that had gone horribly wrong and I was determined to hold back from giving my heart to him again for the foreseeable future. Part of me wanted to hurt him, to show how much he had hurt me, by failing to be my knight in shining armour. If he had tried to reason with Mum as a proper man would have done, then she may have softened and let us keep Nicole. After all, he had a steady job, and we could have made it work like many other teenagers we knew. Once again, I tried to cast aside those negative thoughts and look to the future. It worked for a while.

On the day of the festival, as most always happens, the heavens opened but nothing could dampen our spirits. I was so excited to be going away with Bert and persuaded myself that we would simply be a happy couple at a pop festival. We would be anonymous and the same as lots of other people there: people who had problems of their own, intent on casting them aside for a long weekend and being transported by music into a happier world.

Our journey, if a trifle wet, went well. Howard dropped us off just before the roundabout, complete with a two-man tent he loaned to Bert, and we hitched from there to the festival. Hand in hand, we wandered around the site with our bags on our backs in the pouring rain and waited for the music to begin.

The next morning, after a cold and damp night huddled together in our tiny tent, we plodged through a sea of mud to get something to eat. The rain eased somewhat and after we watched in awe as brilliant bands like Nazareth and Roxy Music performed, nightfall closed in and the light shows began. We headed to the beer tent and bought a couple of beers each, racing back to our tent as the heavens opened again.

I blame the rain. If it had not been for the rain, we would not have been confined to our tent, peering out watching *Slade* and trying to keep dry. If we had not been in our tent, I would not have felt trapped by the insecurity I felt sitting next to Bert. If I had not felt trapped, I would have looked harder for our tent on returning from the toilet. I blame the rain.

On my way back through the crowds I got lost in a sea of tents. There were hundreds of small khaki-brown, canvas tents dotted about, all full of people trying to keep dry with their tent flaps open, watching the bands. It was pitch black, it was wet and it was a simple mistake to make. Suddenly I spotted what I thought was our tent and ran through the mud towards it, flinging myself inside, head first.

'Well, hello there,' said an unfamiliar voice, 'Do you come here often?'

I straightened myself up as far as the tent would allow, to see a face that was unfamiliar too. A face that looked like a pop star. His perfect white teeth were smiling at me and bright blue eyes were staring into my own from underneath a mop of long brown corkscrew curls as he silently offered me a bottle of beer. I declined, blurting out I was in the wrong tent, but he asked me to sit down for a while until the rain eased.

Where's the harm in that? I thought and accepted his offer. After all, it was bucketing down, and I was completely lost.

He held out his hand towards me in fake formality, shaking it as he said, 'I'm Steve from Immingham,' and then looked me up and down and added, 'Are you a Lincoln angel…come to save me from my sins?'

'And what sins would they be, sir?' I asked, joining in with his humour. He just smiled with a wink. I introduced myself and told him I was at the festival with my boyfriend and seemed to have got lost on my way back from the toilet.

'I'm *so* glad you did,' he said.

We started chatting, and soon after his friend, Jess, appeared in the doorway of the tent asking for a bottle of beer. His eyes opened wide in surprise and Steve told him I was a festival vision come to bring glad tidings to all people from Immingham. We all laughed, and it felt good.

Maybe I'll have one beer with them, I decided. *Bert's watching Slade anyway so he won't be worried.*

Four beers and two cannabis joints later, and looking into blue eyes that held no dreadful memories for me, I found I was enjoying myself and the pain inside was diminishing. By the time I came back down to earth it was nearly morning. It was still pouring down and I was persuaded to stay in that unknown tent with those unknown people for a little longer. It was a relief to be with someone new that was not linked to Nicole or the past. It was wonderful to forget for a moment. Until daylight arrived, of course.

I had fallen asleep and, as soon as I opened my eyes and realised where I was, I made a move to go. Steve and Jess both woke up with a start and once again I was asked to stay for a while longer and I agreed. After all, they had been perfect gentlemen in their own way. All they offered me was a place to shelter from the rain … and a few beers … and a couple of joints, but nothing more. Steve went to get us breakfast from one of the food tents and while he was away Jess chatted to me without judgement of any description. He was simply getting to know me for who I was on that day. No talk of the past. No talk of the future. Just chatting.

After breakfast, Steve winked at Jess and asked him to disappear for a while. He took my hand in his and gently stroked it, asking if I would consider going back to Immingham with him. I pulled my hand away, knowing it was wrong to even contemplate what he was saying, but immediately knew this was my escape route from the past. He put his arm around me and looked me straight in the eye, explaining in his strong Lincolnshire accent, 'I've been a scaffolder for four years now. I earn good money and I promise I'll look after you. I've been planning on getting my own place but until I clapped eyes on you, I didn't have a reason. I live with my Auntie Joan and she would be over the moon to see the back of me.'

He stopped talking and put his little finger under my chin and tilted it towards his face, adding, 'I already know I'm in love with you. I knew it as soon as you appeared head first and wringing wet.'

I couldn't believe what he was saying and the escape route from all the memories was becoming a plausible highway. I was in such a state over losing Nicole and already dreaded having to face the consequences day after day for the rest of my life, so I began to weigh up the chance of happiness that Steve from Immingham was offering me. My mind wandered back to reality: *Where's Bert? I have to go and to find him. I can't do this to him.*

Two voices began to battle inside my head. The First Voice was telling me to get out of that tent post-haste and ignore the handsome stranger. 'Go and find Bert. Face up to your responsibilities and carry on with the life you know,' it said.

What responsibilities? I thought. *I don't have any now that Nicole's gone.*

The Second Voice kicked in, booting the other voice to the side.

'It serves Bert right. He was given the chance to claim you as his and he walked past that chance without a care in the world. Go on, Anne, hurt him like he's hurt you!'

Which voice should I listen to? I hadn't a clue. My mind was in enough of a muddle, so for Steve to offer me a new life seemed like a wonderful idea to me at that moment in time.

It all sounded so comforting and even more of a possibility after our first joint of the day. This was the first time I had come across any kind of drugs in my life and, just like the laughing the evening before, it felt good. The joint relaxed me completely and took me to another place. All my life I had been subject to such intense scrutiny from Mum that I had learned to be constantly on guard and on edge … You must know that by now if you've come through all the chapters of the journey with me. Recently of course, I had not relaxed at all, as I was full of shame because of my own actions, so to be able to lay back and listen to the bands playing some of the songs that had helped me through my life so far, was amazing.

Hours and hours of indecision went by and soon it was nightfall again. I had only left Steve's tent twice that day to go to the toilet, and on my return, Steve's purple-fringed scarf was tied to one of the tent poles, guiding me back. As I made my way to the toilets each time, I scoured the site for our tent and was convinced Bert had gone. It was nowhere in sight.

That made me feel better in a strange kind of way, knowing that he had given up on me for the second time and I could move on.

That night, I stayed in the stranger's tent once more, and he held me close as we went to sleep. Jess came and went and eventually came back again in the early hours of the third day and fell asleep too. *Peace, man, peace.*

The next day my doubts returned, and I offered to get breakfast for us all as an excuse to look for Bert again.

How can I do this to him? Even if it was over, he deserved an explanation.

'What!' said The Second Voice invading my head, 'Why ...? Did he give you one when he chose not to stand by you?'

With the voices fighting inside my head, I scoured the site a final time for our tent, but it was a hopeless task and The Second Voice in my head won the battle, fair and square.

Breakfast trays in hand, I headed back to Steve's tent. He suggested we leave the festival that day as we were all soaked to the skin and his tent was leaking badly. 'I'll phone Auntie Joan before we set off to make sure it's alright. There's a phone box in Bardney I saw on the way here.' Before I could speak, he added, 'It'll be fine. You'll see.'

It was as if it was all agreed and I went along with the flow because Steve was very handsome and persuasive. *He's pushier than Bert,* I remember thinking.

Putting it to the back of my mind, I made an instant decision. Bert was in the past and could not hurt me any more. I was moving on to pastures new. The added bonus was that if I went home with Steve, I could hurt Mum at the same time as hurting Bert. I could pelt her with the hurt she had given me to deal with for the rest of my life. Remembering that day at Falloden when she watched blank-faced as I signed the forms to give up my baby, I knew that one day I would get her back. It would serve her right for treating me like a possession all my life without any affection, love or compassion. So, Immingham it was to be, then.

Jess dropped us off at Auntie Joan's place and she welcomed me as if it was normal for her nephew to bring girls to stay. We were only there long enough for each of us to have a bath and get into some dry clothes, then Steve suggested that we go to his local pub. He said there was a bank holiday disco on, and it would be fun.

'Oh, and I've rung the boss and told him I need two more days off. I'll show you round town tomorrow and we can look for a place to live.'

I shuddered. This was all too fast for me, but there was a plus point in that it was well away from home. I was in some kind of ongoing dream or on the verge of a mental breakdown and I was prepared to let them show me where it would lead.

Jess was already there when Steve and I arrived at the pub, and he topped our table up all evening with drink after drink. I was introduced to something called *Gold Label* barley wine which came in a small brown bottle with a gold label, funnily enough. Although it was a beer and I was not used to drinking beer at all, it was lovely. A bit like rocket fuel and, within no time at all, the disco floor beckoned me to dance. Steve seemed content to chat to Jess as I guess they had done for years, having known each other since primary school. I was content to dance and dance in my ongoing dream. I swirled and twirled and smiled at Steve while my drunken emotions switched between feeling deliriously happy and utterly sad. Once again, I was on the edge of the precipice, but for now, I was backing off and letting go. The disco ended suddenly when a fight broke out and everyone was herded out of the pub.

I passed out fully clothed on Auntie's Joan's sofa bed in the lounge, and woke up with a banging head late the next morning.

'This is not the solution,' The First Voice told me.

Immediately, the voice was drowned out by Steve's voice shouting from the kitchen that breakfast was ready. The smell of eggs wafting through made me want to vomit and when I saw the wobbly bits around the yolk, I was not sure how I would keep them down.

'Thank you,' I said weakly as I took the plate out of his hands, 'how did you know I liked eggs?'

'Everybody likes eggs,' he said and winked at me.

What a strange thing for him to say. Most people would have brushed this statement to one side but, having been controlled all my life, it made me take a step back realising here was another controller waiting in the wings.

As I forced the wobbly eggs down my throat, Steve told me that Auntie Joan had gone to work, apparently sneaking past me as I lay in a stupor on the sofa. Not a very good impression to make on your first night.

After breakfast, Steve suggested we should go into Immingham and start looking for somewhere to live. I came to my senses, woke up from my dream and put my foot down. Once my foot was well and truly down, having explained that I needed time to get to know him better, he took me in his arms and told me he would wait for ever if need be.

The arms that had felt so right at the festival now felt so wrong. I was not ready for anything like this. I was far too emotionally wounded. I was deeply scarred and full of sorrow and I wanted to go home. With all the hatred I held inside for Mum, I still knew she had to be told where I was to stop her worrying, as I had been missing for a whole night now after 'staying' at Sue's.

Where will I say I've been? I thought. The First Voice in my head made a welcome return. 'You'll have to tell the truth and face the consequences. And Bert. What about Bert?'

The Second Voice inside my head butted in, 'He'll be back home by now and it's time for you to move on. Forget those blue eyes of his that you don't trust anymore. He'll survive. He'll have to.'

Instead of looking for a place to live, Steve offered to show me around Immingham, ready for when I agreed to move in with him. We walked miles around town, and I felt dreadful all morning. *That's the last time I drink barley wine,* I thought.

That afternoon, I asked Steve to take me to a phone box as I wanted total privacy when I rang Mum. It was the only way to find the strength to spout forth with some conditions before telling her where I was. Conditions I should have voiced a long time ago.

Mum answered immediately and her opening line was, 'Oh Anne, where on earth are you? I've been so worried.'

That threw me somewhat, as her words were an admission that she actually cared for me. I remained strong and true to the promise I had made to myself. I poured out my conditions, word after word, sentence after sentence, almost without taking a breath.

'I'm only going to tell you where I am if you promise not to shout, like you always do. Promise not to judge me. Promise to listen for a change, because you never do. I'm safe and I'm with a boy called Steve that I met at Lincoln Festival. I've been so down after Falloden and you never even noticed. All you do is shout and scream and always say 'no' to everything. I just want some freedom to be myself. I'll never be the perfect daughter you want but *I am* your daughter. You adopted me, remember?'

I paused, and when there was no reply I added, 'There now, I've said it.'

Her voice came down the line and I swear I could hear tears in it as her reply came out in one fell swoop, too.

'Come home, Anne, and we'll have a good talk about what you've just said. Uncle Fred thinks I've been far too strict on you, especially since your dad died. I've always expected far too much and that's why you are the way you are. I'm sorry.'

I was stunned by what she had just said and blurted out Steve's address. As soon as she wrote it down, she added, 'I'm coming to get you.'

'When?' I asked.

'Right now, with Uncle Fred.'

I was over a hundred miles from home, and they were coming to get me at the drop of a hat. I felt more ashamed than before, if that was possible, and realised I had done wrong in trying to run away from the destruction I had caused.

'Face up to your responsibilities …'

The First Voice had eventually won.

Steve and I said our 'goodbyes' before they arrived and we promised to write to each other until I was ready to be with him. I already knew that

would not happen as he seemed like a stranger that day – and anyway …
he had no idea how to cook eggs ….

I wanted to get out of there and go home. Back to the only life I had
ever known, hoping that Mum meant what she said.

'Don't trust anyone, least of all her,' said The Second Voice.

('American Pie' – Don Mclean – 1971)

('Broken Down Angel' – Nazareth – 1973)

I COULD

NO LONGER COPE.

MY WORLD HAD BEEN

TURNED UPSIDE DOWN.

22
The Mess (The Gibbering Wreck)

The Second Voice was right. Mum's promise of a good talk was forgotten after I got home from Immingham, and she continued to treat me like an unwanted burden. In the weeks that followed, I questioned her control more and more as I was still expected to ask for permission to meet up with my friends. She had the power to say 'yay' or 'nay', depending on her mood at the time and whether I pulled my weight with jobs around the house. I knew that. She knew that I knew, and so many jobs were thrown at me which were not usually expected of a teenager. It was blackmail and it went something like this: 'Be the perfect daughter, do everything I ask, and I may allow you some of what you want.'

There was still no sign of love. Her smiles were few and far between and on the rare occasions that I engaged in any conversation with her, the blank expression on her face beautifully illustrated the boredom she felt and told me she was desperate for me to stop talking and leave her alone. We also argued incessantly about almost anything as I became more headstrong, and I took to avoiding her whenever possible. I was at the lowest point in my life and 'Dad's cloud' was still the only outlet I had.

Apart from the misery at home, another battle was raging inside me. A battle between love and hate. Bert was out of the picture because of my behaviour in Lincoln. Even if he forgave me, how could I ever reconcile our relationship when all I wanted to do was to pummel his chest with the inner strength I had left, to try and make him understand how sad and close to the edge I was. If that failed, then my next plan was to boot him in the balls to make sure he could never get another girl pregnant and have her drowning in grief like I was. Hate was dripping from my fingertips. They wanted to claw at Bert and make him understand.

The happy memories of our love invaded another part of my head, and a voice was pleading with me to understand that throughout our years together, Bert had been my protector. He had picked me up on time for our dates, walked me safely home on time, on most occasions, and made sure I was safe in his company. He had put up with my wild spirit but kept it tethered firmly to him. I loved him with all my heart but at the same time I hated him for what he had failed to do. Now we were apart, and I was left wondering if I would ever see him again and how I would feel if I did.

I can describe myself at that point in my life with all the clever adjectives taught to me at the grammar school, but none suffice. Basically, I was a mess. A gibbering wreck.

'The Mess' that I was needed to find a solution to cope with everything that had happened in my life – and find it quickly. I was at a loss where to look. I was going downhill fast. From being disposed of at birth and adopted by a female tyrant, to having no identity of my own, apart from inheriting breasts the size of jugs, had made me constantly question my worth in my younger years. Then, at fourteen, Dad was taken away, leaving me with only his cloud to talk to. Soon after, my first love had shown me I was not worth fighting for and neither was the baby that, after nine safe months in my womb, had been taken away from me. I no longer knew how to bounce back from it all.

Nowadays, I would no doubt have been labelled as going through brief psychotic episodes along with PTSD, brought on by sorrow, grief and anger, and counsellors would have rushed towards me. Then, I was simply labelled as going off the rails, with no one to turn to, and I could not cope. Grief gnaws away at you and wants to cause mayhem and chaos, and it did a good job on me. At its worst, a blind rage reaches down deep inside you telling you to explode and there's the psychotic episode lying in wait, ready to take over.

I am sure if there had been any sign of love and affection in my life at that point in time, if only from Mum, I would have chosen a different path and not the path 'The Mess' took. I wanted love and reassurance. I wanted arms to hold me and tell me that everything would be alright. I wanted someone to want me completely, if only for a moment in time, and even if it was not quite true, it would do. Anyone would do. Just to feel wanted and to belong. Totally belong.

And so, as you journey with me and reach the conclusion of my younger years, I must tell you that in the summer of 1972, 'The Mess' lowered her head once more and teetered towards the edge of the precipice … with the power of hope, resilience and determination reaching out to ambush her, grab hold of her arms and guide her back to safety.

('Seagull' – Bad Company – 1974)

('The Wall in my Head' – Max Harwood, lead actor from 'Jamie' – 2018)

('The Tracks of My Tears' – Smokey Robinson and The Miracles – 1965)

('This Wheel's On Fire' – Julie Driscoll/Brian Auger & The Trinity 1968)

A Big Thank You - From Me to You

Now that you have reached the conclusion of my younger years,

I would love to hear from you.

Send the word '**Finished**' to me,

and I will deliver

a sneaky peek

of

'Survival Without Roots' – Book Two,

straight to your inbox.

(Find out what happens to 'The Mess').

Please contact me by email: anna@annaandersonbooks.com

or

Via the 'Contact' page on my website –www.annaandersonbooks.com

It would be fabulous if you left a review there of

'Survival Without Roots' – Book One.